# The Wisdom of
# William Walker Atkinson

# The Wisdom of
# William Walker Atkinson

By William Walker Atkinson

The Law of Attraction
Practical Mental Influence
The Power of Concentration

# The Law of Attraction

or Thought Vibration in the Thought World

## Table of Contents

# The Universe Is Governed by Law

The Universe is governed by Law — one great Law. Its manifestations are multiform, but viewed from the Ultimate there is but one Law. We are familiar with some of its manifestations, but are almost totally ignorant of certain others. Still we are learning a little more every day — the veil is being gradually lifted.

We speak learnedly of the Law of Gravitation, but ignore that equally wonderful manifestation, *the Law of Attraction in the Thought World*. We are familiar with that wonderful manifestation of Law which draws and holds together the atoms of which matter is composed — we recognize the power of the law that attracts bodies to the earth, that holds the circling worlds in their places, but we close our eyes to the mighty law that draws to us the things we desire or fear, that makes or mars our lives.

When we come to see that Thought is a force — a manifestation of energy — having a magnet-like power of attraction, we will begin to understand the why and wherefore of many things that have heretofore seemed dark to us. There is no study that will so well repay the student for his time and trouble as the study of the workings of this mighty law of the world of Thought — the Law of Attraction.

When we think we send out vibrations of a fine ethereal substance, which are as real as the vibrations manifesting light, heat, electricity, magnetism. That these vibrations are not evident to our five senses is no proof that they do not exist. A powerful magnet will send out vibrations and exert a force sufficient to attract to itself a piece of steel weighing a hundred pounds, but we can neither see, taste, smell, hear nor feel the mighty force. These thought vibrations, likewise, cannot be seen, tasted, smelled, heard nor felt in the ordinary way; although it is true there are on record cases of persons peculiarly sensitive to psychic impressions who have perceived powerful thought-waves, and very many of us can testify that we have distinctly felt the thought vibrations of others, both whilst in the presence of the sender and at a distance. Telepathy and its kindred phenomena are not idle dreams.

Light and heat are manifested by vibrations of a far lower intensity than those of Thought, but the difference is solely in the rate of vibration. The annals of science throw an interesting light upon this question. Prof. Elisha Gray, an eminent scientist, says in his little book, "The Miracles of Nature":

"There is much food for speculation in the thought that there exist sound-waves that no human ear can hear, and color-waves of light that no eye can see. The long, dark, soundless space between 40,000 and 400,000,000,000,000 vibrations per second, and the infinity of range beyond 700,000,000,000,000 vibrations per second, where light ceases, in the universe of motion, makes it possible to indulge in speculation."

M. M. Williams, in his work entitled "Short Chapters in Science," says:

"There is no gradation between the most rapid undulations or tremblings that produce our sensation of sound, and the slowest of those which give rise to our sensations of gentlest warmth. There is a huge gap between them, wide enough to include another world of motion, all lying between our world of sound and our world of heat and light; and there is no good reason whatever for supposing that matter is incapable of such intermediate activity, or that such activity may not give rise to intermediate sensations, provided there are organs for taking up and sensifying their movements."

I cite the above authorities merely to give you food for thought, not to attempt to demonstrate to you the fact that thought vibrations exist. The last-named fact has been fully established to the satisfaction of numerous investigators of the subject, and a little reflection will show you that it coincides with your own experiences.

We often hear repeated the well-known Mental Science statement, "Thoughts are Things," and we say these words over without consciously realizing just what is the meaning of the statement. If we fully comprehended the truth of the statement and the natural consequences of the truth back of it, we should understand many things which have appeared dark to us, and would be able to use the wonderful power, Thought Force, just as we use any other manifestation of Energy.

As I have said, when we think we set into motion vibrations of a very high degree, but just as real as the vibrations of light, heat, sound, electricity. And when we understand the laws governing the production and transmission of these vibrations we will be able to use them in our daily life, just as we do the better known forms of energy. That we cannot see, hear, weigh or measure these vibrations is no proof that they do not exist. There exist waves of sound which no human ear can hear, although some of these are undoubtedly registered by the ear of some of the insects, and others are caught by delicate scientific instruments invented by man; yet there is a great gap between the sounds registered by the most delicate instrument and the limit which man's mind, reasoning by analogy, knows to be the boundary line between sound waves and some other forms of vibration. And there are light waves which the eye of man does not register, some of which may be detected by more delicate instruments, and many more so fine that the instrument has not yet been invented which will detect them, although improvements are being made every year and the unexplored field gradually lessened.

As new instruments are invented, new vibrations are registered by them — and yet the vibrations were just as real before the invention of the instrument as afterward. Supposing that we had no instruments to register magnetism — one might be justified in denying the existence of that mighty force, because it could not be tasted, felt, smelt, heard, seen, weighted or measured. And yet the mighty magnet would still send out waves of force sufficient to draw to it pieces of steel weighing hundreds of pounds.

Each form of vibration requires its own form of instrument for registration. At present the human brain seems to be the only instrument capable of registering thought waves, although occultists say that in this century scientists will invent apparatus sufficiently delicate to catch and register such impressions. And from present indications it looks as if the invention named might be expected at any time. The demand exists and undoubtedly will be soon supplied. But to those who have experimented along the lines of practical telepathy no further proof is required than the results of their own experiments.

We are sending out thoughts of greater or less intensity all the time, and we are reaping the results of such thoughts. Not only do our thought waves influence ourselves and others, but they have a drawing power — they attract to us the thoughts of others, things, circumstances, people, "luck," in accord with the character of the thought uppermost in our minds. Thoughts of Love will attract to us the Love of others; circumstances and surroundings in accord with the thought; people who are of like thought. Thoughts of Anger, Hate, Envy, Malice and Jealousy will draw to us the foul brood of kindred thoughts emanating from the minds of others; circumstances in which we will be called upon to manifest these vile thoughts and will receive them in turn from others; people who will manifest inharmony; and so on. A strong thought or a thought long continued, will make us the center of attraction for the corresponding thought waves of others. Like attracts like in the Thought World — as ye sow so shall ye reap. Birds of a feather flock together in the Thought World — curses like chickens come home to roost, and bringing their friends with them.

The man or woman who is filled with Love sees Love on all sides and attracts the Love of others. The man with hate in his heart gets all the

Hate he can stand. The man who thinks Fight generally runs up against all the Fight he wants before he gets through. And so it goes, each gets what he calls for over the wireless telegraphy of the Mind. The man who rises in the morning feeling "grumpy" usually manages to have the whole family in the same mood before the breakfast is over. The "nagging" woman generally finds enough to gratify her "nagging" propensity during the day.

This matter of Thought Attraction is a serious one. When you stop to think of it you will see that a man really makes his own surroundings, although he blames others for it. I have known people who understood this law to hold a positive, calm thought and be absolutely unaffected by the inharmony surrounding them. They were like the vessel from which the oil had been poured on the troubled waters — they rested safely and calmly whilst the tempest raged around them. One is not at the mercy of the fitful storms of Thought after he has learned the workings of the Law.

We have passed through the age of physical force on to the age of intellectual supremacy, and are now entering a new and almost unknown field, that of psychic power. This field has its established laws and we should acquaint ourselves with them or we will be crowded to the wall as are the ignorant on the planes of effort. I will endeavor to make plain to you the great underlying principles of this new field of energy which is opening up before us, that you may be able to make use of this great power and apply it for legitimate and worthy purposes, just as men are using steam, electricity and other forms of energy today.

# Thought Waves and their Process of Reproduction

Like a stone thrown into the water, thought produces ripples and waves which spread out over the great ocean of thought. There is this difference, however: the waves on the water move only on a level plane in all directions, whereas thought waves move in all directions from a common center, just as do the rays from the sun.

Just as we here on earth are surrounded by a great sea of air, so are we surrounded by a great sea of Mind. Our thought waves move through this vast mental ether, extending, however, in all directions, as I have explained, becoming somewhat lessened in intensity according to the distance traversed, because of the friction occasioned by the waves coming in contact with the great body of Mind surrounding us on all sides.

These thought waves have other qualities differing from the waves on the water. They have the property of reproducing themselves; in this respect they resemble sound waves rather than waves upon the water. Just as a note of the violin will cause the thin glass to vibrate and "sing," so will a strong thought tend to awaken similar vibrations in minds attuned to receive it. Many of the "stray thoughts" which come to us are but reflections or answering vibrations to some strong thought sent out by another. But unless our minds are attuned to receive it, the thought will not likely affect us. If we are thinking high and great thoughts, our minds acquire a certain keynote corresponding to the character of the thoughts we have been thinking. And, this keynote once established, we will be apt to catch the vibrations of other minds keyed to the same thought. On the other hand, let us get into the habit of thinking thoughts of an opposite character, and we will soon be echoing the low order of thought emanating from the minds of the thousands thinking along the same lines.

We are largely what we have thought ourselves into being, the balance being represented by the character of the suggestions and thought of others, which have reached us either directly by verbal suggestions or telepathically by means of such thought waves. Our general mental attitude, however, determines the character of the thought waves received from others as well as the thoughts emanating from ourselves. We receive only such thoughts as are in harmony with the general mental attitude held by ourselves; the thoughts not in harmony affecting us very little, as they awaken no response in us.

The man who believes thoroughly in himself and maintains a positive strong mental attitude of Confidence and Determination is not likely to be affected by the adverse and negative thoughts of Discouragement and Failure emanating from the minds of other persons in whom these last qualities predominate. At the same time these negative thoughts, if they reach one whose mental attitude is pitched on a low key, deepen his negative state and add fuel to the fire which is consuming his strength, or, if you prefer this figure, serve to further smother the fire of his energy and activity.

We attract to us the thoughts of others of the same order of thought. The man who thinks success will be apt to get into tune with the minds of others thinking likewise, and they will help him, and he them. The man who allows his mind to dwell constantly upon thoughts of failure brings himself into close touch with the minds of other "failure" people, and each will tend to pull the other down still more. The man who thinks that all is evil is apt to see much evil, and will be brought into contact with others who will seem to prove his theory. And the man who looks for good in everything and everybody will be likely to attract to himself the things and people corresponding to his thought. We generally see that for which we look.

You will be able to carry this idea more clearly if you will think of the Marconi wireless instruments, which receive the vibrations only from the sending instrument which has been attuned to the same key, while other telegrams are passing through the air in near vicinity without affecting the instrument. The same law applies to the operations of thought. We receive only that which corresponds to our mental attunement. If we have been discouraged, we may rest assured that we have dropped into a negative key, and have been affected not only by our own thoughts but have also received the added depressing thoughts of similar character which are constantly being sent out from the minds of other unfortunates who have not yet learned the law of attraction in the thought world. And if we occasionally rise to heights of enthusiasm and energy, how quickly we feel the inflow of the courageous, daring, energetic, positive thoughts being sent out by the live men and women of the world. We recognize this without much trouble when we come in personal contact with people and feel their vibrations, depressing or invigorating, as the case may be. But the same law operates when we are not in their presence, although less strongly.

The mind has many degrees of pitch, ranging from the highest positive note to the lowest negative note, with many notes in between, varying in pitch according to their respective distance from the positive or negative extreme.

When your mind is operating along positive lines you feel strong, buoyant, bright, cheerful, happy, confident and courageous, and are enabled to do your work well, to carry out your intentions, and progress on your roads to Success. You send out strong positive thought, which affects others and causes them to cooperate with you or to follow your lead, according to their own mental keynote.

When you are playing on the extreme negative end of the mental keyboard you feel depressed, week, passive, dull, fearful, cowardly. And you find yourself unable to make progress or to succeed. And your effect upon others is practically nil. You are led by, rather than leading others, and are used as a human doormat or football by more positive persons.

In some persons the positive element seems to predominate, and in others the negative quality seems to be more in evidence. There are, of course, widely varying degrees of positiveness and negativeness, and B may be negative to A, while positive to C. When two people first meet there is generally a silent mental conflict in which their respective minds test their quality of positiveness, and fix their relative position toward each other. This process may be unconscious in many cases, but it occurs nevertheless. The adjustment is often automatic, but occasionally the struggle is so sharp — the opponents being so well matched — that the matter forces itself into the consciousness of the two people. Sometimes both parties are so much alike in their degrees of positiveness that they fail to come to terms, mentally; they never really are able to get along with each other, and they are either mutually repelled and separate or else stay together amid constant broils and wrangling.

We are positive or negative to everyone with whom we have relations. We may be positive to our children, our employees and dependents, but we are at the same time negative to others to whom we occupy inferior positions, or whom we have allowed to assert themselves over us.

Of course, something may occur and we will suddenly become more positive than the man or woman to whom we have heretofore been negative. We frequently see cases of this kind. And as the knowledge of these mental laws becomes more general we will see many more instances of persons asserting themselves and making use of their newfound power.

But remember you possess the power to raise the keynote of your mind to a positive pitch by an effort of the will. And, of course, it is equally true that you may allow yourself to drop into a low, negative note by carelessness or a weak will.

There are more people on the negative plane of thought than on the positive plane, and consequently there are more negative thought vibrations in operation in our mental atmosphere. But, happily for us, this is counterbalanced by the fact that a positive thought is infinitely more powerful than a negative one, and if by force of will we raise ourselves to a higher mental key we can shut out the depressing thoughts and may take up the vibrations corresponding with our changed mental attitude. This is one of the secrets of the affirmations and autosuggestions used by the several schools of Mental Science and other New Thought cults. There is no particular merit in affirmations of themselves, but they serve a twofold purpose: (1) They tend to establish new mental attitudes within us and act wonderfully in the direction of character- building — the science of making ourselves over. (2) They tend to raise the mental keynote so that we may get the benefit of the positive thought waves of others on the same plane of thought.

Whether or not we believe in them, we are constantly making affirmations. The man who asserts that he can and will do a thing — and asserts it earnestly — develops in himself the qualities conducive to the well doing of that thing, and at the same time places his mind in the proper key to receive all the thought waves likely to help him in the doing. If, on the other hand, one says and feels that he is going to fail, he will choke and smother the thoughts coming from his own subconscious mentality which are intended to help him, and at the same time will place himself in tune with the Failure—thought of the world — and there is plenty of the latter kind of thought around, I can tell you.

Do not allow yourselves to be affected by the adverse and negative thoughts of those around you. Rise to the upper chambers of your mental dwelling, and key yourself up to a strong pitch, away above the vibrations on the lower planes of thought. Then you will not only be immune to their negative vibrations but will be in touch with the great body of strong positive thought coming from those of your own plane of development. My aim will be to direct and train you in the proper use of thought and will, that you may have yourself well in hand and may be able to strike the positive key at any moment you may feel it necessary. It is not necessary to strike the extreme note on all occasions. The better plan is to keep yourself in a comfortable key, without much strain, and to have the means at command whereby you can raise the pitch at once when occasion demands. By this knowledge you will not be at the mercy of the old automatic action of the mind, but may have it well under your own control.

Development of the will is very much like the development of a muscle — a matter of practice and gradual improvement. At first it is apt to be tiresome, but at each trial one grows stronger until the new strength becomes real and permanent. Many of us have made ourselves positive under sudden calls or emergencies. We are in the habit of "bracing up" when occasion demands. But by intelligent practice you will be so much strengthened that your habitual state will be equal to your "bracing up" stage now, and then when you find it necessary to apply the spur you will be able to reach a stage not dreamed of at present.

Do not understand me as advocating a high tension continuously. This is not at all desirable, not only because it is apt to be too much of a strain upon you but also because you will find it desirable to relieve the tension at times and become receptive that you may absorb impressions. It is well to be able to relax and assume a certain degree of receptiveness, knowing that you are always able to spring back to the more positive state at will. The habitually strongly positive man loses much enjoyment and recreation. Positive, you give out expressions; receptive, you take in impressions. Positive, you are a teacher; receptive, a pupil. It is not only a good thing to be a good teacher, but it is also very important to be a good listener at times.

# A Talk About the Mind

Man has but one mind, but he has many mental faculties, each faculty being capable of functioning along two different lines of mental effort. There are no distinct dividing lines separating the two several functions of a faculty, but they shade into each other as do the colors of the spectrum.

An Active effort of any faculty of the mind is the result of a direct impulse imparted at the time of the effort. A Passive effort of any faculty of the mind is the result of either a preceding Active effort of the same mind; an Active effort of another along the lines of suggestion; Thought Vibrations from the mind of another; Thought impulses from an ancestor, transmitted by the laws of heredity (including impulses transmitted from generation to generation from the time of the original vibratory impulse imparted by the Primal Cause — which impulses gradually unfold, and unsheath, when the proper state of evolutionary development is reached).

The Active effort is new-born — fresh from the mint, whilst the Passive effort is of less recent creation, and, in fact, is often the result of vibratory impulses imparted in ages long past. The Active effort makes its own way, brushing aside the impeding vines and kicking from its path the obstructing stones. The Passive effort travels along the beaten path.

A thought-impulse, or motion-impulse, originally caused by an Active effort of faculty, may become by continued repetition, or habit, strictly automatic, the impulse given it by the repeated Active effort developing a strong momentum, which carries it on, along Passive lines, until stopped by another Active effort or its direction changed by the same cause.

On the other hand, thought-impulses, or motion-impulses, continued along Passive lines may be terminated or corrected by an Active effort. The Active function creates, changes or destroys. The Passive function carries on the work given it by the Active function and obeys orders and suggestions.

The Active function produces the thought-habit, or motion-habit, and imparts to it the vibrations, which carry it on along the Passive lines thereafter. The Active function also has the power to send forth vibrations which neutralize the momentum of the thought-habit, or motion-habit; it also is able to launch a new thought-habit, or motion-habit, with stronger vibrations, which overcomes and absorbs the first thought, or motion, and substitutes the new one.

All thought-impulses, or motion-impulses, once started on their errands, continue to vibrate along passive lines until corrected or terminated by subsequent impulses imparted by the Active function, or other controlling power. The continuance of the original impulse adds momentum and force to it, and renders its correction or termination more difficult. This explains that which is called "the force of habit." I think that this will be readily understood by those who have struggled to overcome a habit which had been easily acquired. The Law applies to good habits as well as bad. The moral is obvious.

Several of the faculties of the mind often combine to produce a single manifestation. A task to be performed may call for the combined exercise of several faculties, some of which may manifest by Active effort and others by Passive effort.

The meeting of new conditions — new problems — calls for the exercise of Active effort; whilst a familiar problem, or task, can be easily handled by the Passive effort without the assistance of his more enterprising brother.

There is in Nature an instinctive tendency of living organisms to perform certain actions, the tendency of an organized body to seek that which satisfies the wants of its organism. This tendency is sometimes called Appetency. It is really a Passive mental impulse, originating with the impetus imparted by the Primal Cause, and transmitted along the lines of evolutionary development, gaining strength and power as it progresses. The impulse of the Primal Cause is assisted by the powerful upward attraction exerted by *The Absolute*.

In plant life this tendency is plainly discernible, ranging form the lesser exhibitions in the lower types to the greater in the higher types. It is that which is generally spoken of as the "life-force" in plants. It is, however, a manifestation of rudimentary mentation, functioning along the lines of Passive effort. In some of the higher forms of plant life there appears a faint color of independent "life action" — a faint indication of choice of volition. Writers on plant life relate many remarkable instances of this phenomenon. It is, undoubtedly, an exhibition of rudimentary Active mentation.

In the lower animal kingdom a very high degree of Passive mental effort is found. And, varying in degree in the several families and species, a considerable amount of Active mentation is apparent. The lower animal undoubtedly possesses Reason only in a lesser degree than man, and, in fact, the display of volitional mentation exhibited by an intelligent animal is often nearly as high as that shown by the lower types of man or by a young child.

As a child, before birth, shows in its body the stages of the physical evolution of man, so does a child, before and after birth — until maturity — manifest the stages of the mental evolution of man.

Man, the highest type of life yet produced, at least upon this planet, shows the highest form of Passive mentation, and also a much higher development of Active mentation than is seen in the lower animals, and yet the degrees of that power vary widely among the different races of men. Even among men of our race the different degrees of Active mentation are plainly noticeable; these degrees not depending by any means upon the amount of "culture," social position or educational advantages possessed by the individual: Mental Culture and Mental Development are two very different things.

You have but to look around you to see the different stages of the development of Active mentation in man. The reasoning of many men is scarcely more than Passive mentation, exhibiting but little of the qualities of volitional thought. They prefer to let other men think for them. Active mentation tires them and they find the instinctive, automatic, Passive mental process much easier. Their minds work along the lines of least resistance. They are but little more than human sheep,

Among the lower animals and the lower types of men Active mentation is largely confined to the grosser faculties — the more material plane; the higher mental faculties working along the instinctive, automatic lines of the Passive function.

As the lower forms of life progressed in the evolutionary scale, they developed new faculties which were latent within them. These faculties always manifested in the form of rudimentary Passive functioning, and afterwards worked up through higher Passive forms, until the Active functions were brought into play. The evolutionary process still continues, the invariable tendency being toward the goal of highly developed Active mentation. This evolutionary progress is caused by the vibratory impulse imparted by the Primal Cause, aided by the uplifting attraction of *The Absolute.*

This law of evolution is still in progress, and man is beginning to develop new powers of mind, which, of course, are first manifesting themselves along the lines of Passive effort. Some men have developed these new faculties to a considerable degree, and it is possible that before long Man will be able to exercise them along the line of their Active functions. In fact, this power has already been attained by a few. This is the secret of the Oriental occultists, and of some of their Occidental brethren.

The amenability of the mind to the will can be increased by properly directed practice. That which we are in the habit of referring to as the "strengthening of the Will" is in reality the training of the mind to recognize and absorb the Power Within. The Will is strong enough, it does not need strengthening, but the mind needs to be trained to receive and act upon the suggestions of the Will. The Will is the outward manifestation of the *I Am*. The Will current is flowing in full strength along the spiritual wires; but you must learn how to raise the trolley-pole to touch it before the mental car will move. This is a somewhat different idea from that which you have been in the habit of receiving from writers on the subject of Will Power, but it is correct, as you will demonstrate to your own satisfaction if you will follow up the subject by experiments along the proper lines.

The attraction of *The Absolute* is drawing man upward, and the vibratory force of the Primal Impulse has not yet exhausted itself. The time of evolutionary development has come when man can help himself. The man who understands the Law can accomplish wonders by means of the development of the powers of the mind; whilst the man who turns his back upon the truth will suffer from his lack of knowledge of the Law.

He who understands the laws of his mental being, develops his latent powers and uses them intelligently. He does not despise his Passive mental functions, but makes good use of them also, charges them with the duties for which they are best fitted, and is able to obtain wonderful results from their work, having mastered them and trained them to do the bidding of the Higher Self. When they fail to do their work properly he regulates them, and his knowledge prevents him from meddling with them unintelligently, and thereby doing himself harm. He develops the faculties and powers latent within him and learns how to manifest them along the line of Active mentation as well as Passive. He knows that the real man within him is the master to whom both Active and Passive functions are but tools. He has banished Fear, and enjoys Freedom. He has found himself. *He has learned the secret of the I am.*

# Mind Building

Man can build up his mind and make it what he wills. In fact, we are mind-building every hour of our lives, either consciously or unconsciously. The majority of us are doing the work unconsciously, but those who have seen a little below the surface of things have taken the matter in hand and have become conscious creators of their own mentality. They are no longer subject to the suggestions and influences of others but have become masters of themselves. They assert the "I," and compel obedience from the subordinate mental faculties. The "I" is the sovereign of the mind, and what we call *Will* is the instrument of the "I." Of course, there is something back of this, and the Universal Will is higher than the Will of the Individual, but the latter is in much closer touch with the Universal Will than is generally supposed, and when one conquers the lower self, and asserts the "I," he becomes in close touch with the Universal Will and partakes largely of its wonderful power. The moment one asserts the "I," and "finds himself," he establishes a close connection between the Individual Will and the Universal Will. But before he is able to avail himself of the mighty power at his command, he must first effect the Mastery of the lower self.

Think of the absurdity of Man claiming to manifest powers, when he is the slave of the lower parts of his mental being, which should be subordinate. Think of a man being the slave of his moods, passions, animal appetites and lower faculties, and at the same time trying to claim the benefits of the Will. Now, I am not preaching asceticism, which seems to me to be a confession of weakness. I am speaking of Self-Mastery — the assertion of the "I" over the subordinate parts of oneself. In the higher view of the subject, this "I" is the only real Self, and the rest is the non-self; but our space does not permit the discussion of this point, and we will use the word "self" as meaning the entire man. Before a man can assert the "I" in its full strength he must obtain the complete mastery of the subordinate parts of the self. All things are good when we learn to master them, but no thing is good when it masters us. Just so long as we allow the lower portions of the self to give us orders, we are slaves. It is only when the "I" mounts his throne and lifts the scepter, that order is established and things assume their proper relation to each other.

We are finding no fault with those who are swayed by their lower selves — they are in a lower grade of evolution, and will work up in time. But we are calling the attention of those who are ready, to the fact that the Sovereign must assert his will, and that the subjects must obey. Orders must be given and carried out. Rebellion must be put down, and the rightful authority insisted upon. And the time to do it is Now.

You have been allowing your rebellious subjects to keep the King from his throne. You have been allowing the mental kingdom to be misgoverned by irresponsible faculties. You have been the slaves of Appetite, Unworthy Thoughts, Passion and Negativeness. The Will has been set aside and Low Desire has usurped the throne. It is time to reestablish order in the mental kingdom. You are able to assert the mastery over any emotion, appetite, passion or class of thoughts by the assertion of the Will. You can order Fear to go to the rear; Jealousy to leave your presence; Hate to depart from your sight; Anger to hide itself; Worry to cease troubling you; Uncontrolled Appetite and Passion to bow in submission and to become humble slaves instead of masters — all by the assertion of the "I." You may surround yourself with the glorious company of Courage, Love and Self-Control, by the same means. You may put down the rebellion and secure peace and order in your mental kingdom if you will but utter the mandate and insist upon its execution. Before you march forth to empire, you must establish the proper internal condition — must show your ability to govern you own kingdom. The first battle is the conquest of the lesser self by the Real Self.

**Affirmation**

I *Am* Asserting the Mastery of My Real Self

Repeat these words earnestly and positively during the day at least once an hour, and particularly when you are confronted with conditions which tempt you to act on the lines of the lesser self instead of following the course dictated by the Real Self. In the moment of doubt and hesitation say these words earnestly, and your way will be made clear to you. Repeat them several times after you retire and settle yourself to sleep. But be sure to back up the words with the thought inspiring them, and do not merely repeat them parrot-like. Form the mental image of the Real Self asserting its mastery over the lower planes of your mind — see the King on his Throne. You will become conscious of an influx of new thought, and things which have seemed hard for you will suddenly become much easier. You will feel that you have yourself well in hand, and that *you* are the master and not the slave. The thought you are holding will manifest itself in action, and you will steadily grow to become that which you have in mind.

### Exercise

Fix the mind firmly on the higher Self and draw inspiration from it when you feel led to yield to the promptings of the lower part of your nature. When you are tempted to burst into Anger — assert the "I," and your voice will drop. Anger is unworthy of the developed Self. When you feel vexed and cross, remember what you are, and rise above your feeling. When you feel Fearful, remember that the Real Self fears nothing, and assert Courage. When you feel Jealousy inciting, think of your higher nature, and laugh. And so on, asserting the Real Self and not allowing the things on the lower plane of mentality to disturb you. They are unworthy of you, and must be taught to keep their places. Do not allow these things to master you — they should be your subjects, not your masters. You must get away from this plane, and the only way to do so is to cut loose from these phases of thought which have been "running things" to suit themselves. You may have trouble at the start, but keep at it and you will have that satisfaction which comes only from conquering the lower parts of our nature. You have been a slave long enough — now is the time to free yourselves. If you will follow these exercises faithfully you will be a different being by the end of the year, and will look back with a pitying smile to your former condition. But it takes work. This is not child's play but a task for earnest men and women, Will *you* make the effort?

# The Secret of the Will

While psychologists may differ in their theories regarding the nature of the Will, none deny its existence, nor question its power. All persons recognize the power of strong Will — all see how it may be used to overcome the greatest obstacles. But few realize that the Will may be developed and strengthened by intelligent practice. They feel that they could accomplish wonders if they had a strong Will, but instead of attempting to develop it, they content themselves with vain regrets. They sigh, but do nothing.

Those who have investigated the subject closely know that Will Power, with all its latent possibilities and mighty powers, may be developed, disciplined, controlled and directed, just as may be any other of Nature's forces. It does not matter what theory you may entertain about the nature of the Will, you will obtain the results if you practice intelligently.

Personally, I have a somewhat odd theory about the Will. I believe that every man has, potentially, a strong Will, and that all he has to do is to train his mind to make use of it. I think that in the higher regions of the mind of every man is a great store of Will Power awaiting his use. The Will current is running along the psychic wires, and all that it is necessary to do is to raise the mental trolley-pole and bring down the power for your use. And the supply is unlimited, for your little storage battery is connected with the great powerhouse of the Universal Will Power, and the power is inexhaustible. Your Will does not need training — but your Mind does. The mind is the instrument and the supply of Will Power is proportionate to the fineness of the instrument through which it manifests. But you needn't accept this theory if you don't like it. This lesson will fit your theory as well as mine.

He who has developed his mind so that it will allow the Will Power to manifest through it, has opened up wonderful possibilities for himself. Not only has he found a great power at his command, but he is able to bring into play, and use, faculties, talents and abilities of whose existence he has not dreamed. This secret of the Will is the magic key which opens all doors.

The late Donald G. Mitchell once wrote: "Resolve is what makes a man manifest; not puny resolve, but crude determination; not errant purpose — but that strong and indefatigable will which treads down difficulties and danger, as a boy treads down the heaving frost-lands of winter; which kindles his eye and brain with a proud pulse-beat toward the unattainable. Will makes men giants."

Many of us feel that if we would but exert our Will, we might accomplish wonders. But somehow we do not seem to want to take the trouble — at any rate; we do not get to the actual willing point. We put it off from time to time, and talk vaguely of "some day," but that some day never comes.

We instinctively feel the power of the Will, but we haven't enough energy to exercise it, and so drift along with the tide, unless perhaps some friendly difficulty arises, some helpful obstacle appears in our path, or some kindly pain stirs us into action, in either of which cases we are compelled to assert our Will and thus begin to accomplish something.

The trouble with us is that we do not want to do the thing enough to make us exert our Will Power. We don't want to hard enough. We are mentally lazy and of weak Desire. If you do not like the word Desire substitute for it the word "Aspiration." (Some people call the lower impulses Desires, and the higher, Aspirations — it's all a matter of words, take you choice.) That is the trouble. Let a man be in danger of losing his life — let a woman be in danger of losing a great love — and you will witness a startling exhibition of Will Power from an unexpected source. Let a woman's child be threatened with danger, and she will manifest a degree of Courage and Will that sweeps all before it. And yet the same woman will quail before a domineering husband, and will lack the Will to perform a simple task. A boy will do all sorts of work if he but considers it play, and yet he can scarcely force himself to cut a little firewood. Strong Will follows strong Desire. If you really want to do a thing very much, you can usually develop the Will Power to accomplish it.

The trouble is that you have not really wanted to do these things, and yet you blame your Will. You say that you do want to do it, but if you stop to think you will see that you really want to do something else more than the thing in question. You are not willing to pay the price of attainment. Stop a moment and analyze this statement and apply it in your own case,

You are mentally lazy — that's the trouble. Don't talk to me about not having enough Will. You have a great storehouse of Will awaiting your use, but you are too lazy to use it. Now, if you are really in earnest about this matter, get to work and first find out what you really want to do — then start to work and do it. Never mind about the Will Power — you'll find a full supply of that whenever you need it. The thing to do is to get to the point where you will resolve to do. That the real test — the resolving. Think of these things a little, and make up your mind whether or not you really want to be a Willer sufficiently hard to get to work.

Many excellent essays and books have been written on this subject, all of which agree regarding the greatness of Will Power, the most enthusiastic terms being used; but few have anything to say about how this power may be acquired by those who have it not, or who possess it in but a limited degree. Some have given exercises designed to "strengthen" the Will, which exercises really strengthen the Mind so that it is able to draw upon its store of power. But they have generally overlooked the fact that in autosuggestion is to be found the secret of the development of the mind so that it may become the efficient instrument of the Will.

## Autosuggestion
I *am* Using My Will Power

Say these words several times earnestly and positively, immediately after finishing this article. Then repeat them frequently during the day, at least once an hour, and particularly when you meet something that calls for the exercise of Will Power. Also repeat them several times after you retire and settle yourself for sleep. Now, there is nothing in the words unless you back them up with the thought. In fact, the thought is "the whole thing," and the words only pegs upon which to hang the thought. So think of what you are saying, and mean what you say. You must use Faith at the start, and use the words with a confident expectation of the result. Hold the steady thought that you are drawing on your storehouse of Will Power, and before long you will find that thought is taking form in action, and that your Will Power is manifesting itself. You will feel an influx of strength with each repetition of the words. You will find yourself overcoming difficulties and bad habits, and will be surprised at how things are being smoothed out for you.

## Exercise
Perform at least one disagreeable task each day during the month.. If there is any especially disagreeable task which you would like to shirk, that is the one for you to perform. This is not given to you in order to make you self-sacrificing or meek, or anything of that sort — it is given you to exercise your Will. Anyone can do a pleasant thing cheerfully, but it takes Will to do the unpleasant thing cheerfully; and that is how you must do the work. It will prove a most valuable discipline to you. Try it for a month and you will see where "it comes in." If you shirk this exercise you had better stop right here and acknowledge that you do not want Will Power, and are content to stay where you are and remain a weakling.

# How to Become Immune to Injurious Thought Attraction

The first thing to do is to begin to "cut out" Fear and Worry. Fear-thought is the cause of much unhappiness and many failures. You have been told this thing over and over again, but it will bear repeating. Fear is a habit of mind which has been fastened upon us by negative race-thought, but from which we may free ourselves by individual effort and perseverance.

Strong expectancy is a powerful magnet. He of the strong, confident desire attracts to him the things best calculated to aid him — persons, things circumstances, surroundings; if he desires them hopefully, trustfully, confidently, calmly. And, equally true, he who Fears a thing generally manages to start into operation forces which will cause the thing he feared to come upon him. Don't you see, the man who Fears really expects the feared thing, and the eyes of the Law is the same as if he really had wished for or desired it? The Law is operative in both cases — the principle is the same.

The best way to overcome the habit of Fear is to assume the mental attitude of Courage, just as the best way to get rid of darkness is to let in the light. It is a waste of time to fight a negative thought-habit by recognizing its force and trying to deny it out of existence by mighty efforts. The best, surest, easiest and quickest method is to assume the existence of the positive thought desired in its place; and by constantly dwelling upon the positive thought, manifest it into objective reality.

Therefore, instead of repeating, "I'm not afraid," say boldly, "I am full of Courage," "I am Courageous." You must assert, "There's nothing to fear," which, although in the nature of a denial, simply denies the reality of the object causing fear rather than admitting the fear itself and then denying it.

To overcome fear, one should hold firmly to the mental attitude of Courage. He should think Courage, say Courage, act Courage. He should keep the mental picture of Courage before him all the time, until it becomes his normal mental attitude. Hold the ideal firmly before you and you will gradually grow to its attainment — the ideal will become manifest.

Let the word "Courage" sink deeply into your mind, and then hold it firmly there until the mind fastens it in place. Think of yourself as being Courageous — see yourself as acting with Courage in trying situations. Realize that there is nothing to Fear — that Worry and Fear never helped anyone, and never will. Realize that Fear paralyzes effort, and that Courage promotes activity.

The confident, fearless, expectant, "I Can and I Will" man is a mighty magnet. He attracts to himself just what is needed for his success. Things seem to come his way, and people say he is "lucky." Nonsense! "Luck" has nothing to do with it. It's all in the Mental Attitude. And the Mental Attitude of the "I Can't" or the "I'm Afraid" man also determines his measure of success. There's no mystery whatsoever about it. You have but to look about you to realize the truth of what I have said. Did you ever know a successful man who did not have the "I Can and I will" thought strong within him? Why, he will walk all around the "I Can't" man, who has perhaps even more ability. The first mental attitude brought to the surface latent qualities, as well as attracted help from outside; whilst the second mental attitude not only attracted "I Can't" people and things, but also kept the man's own powers from manifesting themselves. I have demonstrated the correctness of these views, and so have many others, and the number of people who know these things is growing every day.

Don't waste your Thought-Force, but use it to advantage. Stop attracting to yourself failure, unhappiness, inharmony, sorrow — begin now and send out a current of bright, positive, happy thought. Let your prevailing thought be "I Can and I Will;" think "I Can and I Will;" dream "I Can and I Will;" say "I Can and I Will;" and act "I Can and I Will". Live on the "I Can and I and Will" plane, and before you are aware of it, you will feel the new vibrations manifesting themselves in action; will see them bring results; will be conscious of the new point of view; will realize that your own is coming to you. You will feel better, act better, see better, *be* better in every way, after you join the "I Can and I Will" brigade.

Fear is the parent of Worry, Hate, Jealousy, Malice, Anger, Discontent, Failure and all the rest. The man who rids himself of Fear will find that the rest of the brood has disappeared. The only way to be Free is to get rid of Fear. Tear it out by the roots. I regard the conquest of Fear as the first important step to be taken by those who wish to master the application of Thought Force. So long as Fear masters you, you are in no condition to make progress in the realm of Thought, and I must insist that you start to work at once to get rid of this obstruction. You *can* do it — if you only go about it in earnest. And when you have ridded yourself of the vile thing, life will seem entirely different to you — you will feel happier, freer, stronger, more positive, and will be more successful in every undertaking of Life.

Start it today, make up your mind that this intruder must *go* — do not compromise matters with him, but insist upon an absolute surrender on his part. You will find the task difficult at first, but each time you oppose him he will grow weaker, and you will be stronger. Shut off his nourishment — starve him to death — he cannot live in a thought atmosphere of Fearlessness. So, start to fill your mind with good, strong, Fearless thoughts — keep yourself busy thinking Fearlessness, and Fear will die of his own accord. Fearlessness is positive — Fear is negative, and you may be sure that the positive will prevail.

So long as Fear is around with his "but," "if," "suppose," "I'm afraid," "I can't," "what if," and all the rest of his cowardly suggestions, you will not be able to use your Thought Force to the best advantage. Once get him out of the way, you will have clear sailing, and every inch of thought- sail will catch the wind. He is a Jonah. Overboard with him! (The whale that swallows him will have my sympathy.)

I advise that you start in to do some of the things which you feel you could do if you were not afraid to try. Start to work to do these things, affirming Courage all the way through, and you will be surprised to see how the changed mental attitude will clear away obstacles from your path, and will make things very much easier than you had anticipated. Exercises of this kind will develop you wonderfully, and you will be much gratified at the result of a little practice along these lines.

There are many things before you awaiting accomplishment, which you can master if you will only throw aside the yoke of Fear — if you will only refuse to accept the race suggestion, and will boldly assert the "I" and its power. And the best way to vanquish Fear is to assert "Courage" and stop thinking of Fear. By this plan you will train the mind into new habits of thought, thus eradicating the old negative thoughts which have been pulling you down, and holding you back. Take the word "Courage" with you as your watchword and manifest it in action.

Remember, the only thing to fear is Fear, and — well, don't even fear Fear, for he's a cowardly chap at the best, who will run if you show a brave front.

# The Transmutation of Negative Thought

Worry is the child of Fear — if you kill out Fear, Worry will die for want of nourishment. This advice is very old, and yet it is always worthy of repetition, for it is a lesson of which we are greatly in need. Some people think that if we kill out Fear and Worry we will never be able to accomplish anything. I have read editorials in the great journals in which the writers held that without Worry one can never accomplish any of the great tasks of life, because Worry is necessary to stimulate interest and work. This is nonsense, no matter who utters it. Worry never helped one to accomplish anything; on the contrary, it stands in the way of accomplishment and attainment.

The motive underlying action and "doing things" is Desire and Interest. If one earnestly desires a thing, he naturally becomes very much interested in its accomplishment, and is quick to seize upon anything likely to help him to gain the thing he wants. More than that, his mind starts up a work on the subconscious plane that brings into the field of consciousness many ideas of value and importance. Desire and Interest are the causes that result in success. Worry is not Desire. It is true that if one's surroundings and environments become intolerable, he is driven in desperation to some efforts that will result in throwing off the undesirable conditions and in the acquiring of those more in harmony with his desire. But this is only another form of Desire — the man desires something different from what he has; and when his desire becomes strong enough his entire interest is given to the task, he makes a mighty effort, and the change is accomplished. But it wasn't Worry that caused the effort. Worry could content itself with wringing its hands and moaning, "Woe is me," and wearing its nerves to a frazzle, and accomplishing nothing. Desire acts differently. It grows stronger as the man's conditions become intolerable, and finally when he feels the hurt so strongly that he can't stand it any longer, he says, "I won't stand this any longer — l will make a change," and lo! Then Desire springs into action. The man keeps on "wanting" a change the worst way (which is the best way) and his Interest and Attention being given to the task of deliverance, he begins to make things move. Worry never accomplished anything. Worry is negative and death producing. Desire and Ambition are positive and life producing. A man may worry himself to death and yet nothing will be accomplished, but let that man transmute his worry and discontent into Desire and Interest, coupled with a belief that he is able to make the change — the "I Can and I Will" idea — then something happens.

Yes, Fear and Worry must go before we can do much. One must proceed to cast out these negative intruders, and replace them with Confidence and Hope. Transmute Worry into keen Desire. Then you will find that Interest is awakened, and you will begin to think things of interest to you. Thoughts will come to you from the great reserve stock in your mind and you will start to manifest them in action. Moreover you will be placing yourself in harmony with similar thoughts of others, and will draw to you aid and assistance from the great volume of thought waves with which the world is filled. One draws to himself thought waves corresponding in character with the nature of the prevailing thoughts in his won mind — his mental attitude. Then again he begins to set into motion the great Law of Attraction, whereby he draws to him others likely to help him, and is, in turn, attracted to others who can aid him. This Law of Attraction is no joke, no metaphysical absurdity, but is a great live working principle of Nature, as anyone may learn by experimenting and observing.

To succeed in anything you must want it very much — Desire must be in evidence in order to attract. The man of weak desires attracts very little to himself. The stronger the Desire the greater the force set into motion. You must want a thing hard enough before you can get it. You must want it more than you do the things around you, and you must be prepared to pay the price for it. The price is the throwing overboard of certain lesser desires that stand in the way of the accomplishment of the greater one. Comfort, ease, leisure, amusements, and many other things may have to go (not always, though). It all depends on what you want. As a rule, the greater the thing desired, the greater the price to be paid for it. Nature believes in adequate compensation. But if you really Desire a thing in earnest, you will pay the price without question; for the Desire will dwarf the importance of the other things.

You say that you want a thing very much, and are doing everything possible toward its attainment? Pshaw! You are only playing Desire. Do you want the thing as much as a prisoner wants freedom — as much as a dying man wants life? Look at the almost miraculous things accomplished by prisoners desiring freedom. Look how they work through steel plates and stonewalls with a bit of stone. Is your desire as strong as that? Do you work for the desired thing as if your life depended upon it? Nonsense! You don't know what Desire is. I tell you if a man wants a thing as much as the prisoner wants freedom, or as much as a strongly vital man wants life, then that man will be able to sweep away obstacles and impediments apparently immovable. The key to attainment is Desire, Confidence, and Will. This key will open many doors.

Fear paralyzes Desire — it scares the life out of it. You must get rid of Fear. There have been times in my life when Fear would get hold of me and take a good, firm grip on my vitals, and I would lose all hope; all interest; all ambition; all desire. But, thank the Lord, I have always managed to throw off the grip of the monster and face my difficulty like a man; and lo! Things would seem to be straightened out for me somehow. Either the difficulty would melt away or I would be given means to overcome, or get around, or under or over it. It is strange how this works. No matter how great is the difficulty, when we finally face it with courage and confidence in ourselves, we seem to pull through somehow, and then we begin to wonder what we were scared about. This is not a mere fancy, it is the working of a mighty law, which we do not as yet fully understand, but which we may prove at any time.

People often ask: "it's all very well for you New Thought people to say 'Don't worry,' but what's a person to do when he thinks of all the possible things ahead of him, which might upset him and his plans? Well, all that I can say is that the man is foolish to bother about thinking of troubles to come at some time in the future. The majority of things that we worry about don't come to pass at all; a large proportion of the others come in a milder form than we had anticipated, and there are always other things which come at the same time which help us to overcome the trouble. The future holds in store for us not only difficulties to be overcome, but also agents to help us in overcoming the difficulties. Things adjust themselves. We are prepared for any trouble which may come upon us, and when the time comes we somehow find ourselves able to meet it. God not only tempers the wind to the shorn lamb, but He also tempers the shorn lamb to the wind. The winds and the shearing do not come together; there is usually enough time for the lamb to get seasoned, and then he generally grows new wool before the cold blast comes.

It has been well said that nine-tenths of the worries are over things which never comes to pass, and that the other tenth is over things of little or no account. So what's the use in using up all your reserve force in fretting over future troubles, if this be so? Better wait until your troubles really come before you worry. You will find that by this storing up of energy you will be able to meet about any sort of trouble that comes your way.

What is it that uses up all the energy in the average man or woman, anyway? Is it the real overcoming of difficulties, or the worrying about impending troubles? It's always "Tomorrow, tomorrow," and yet tomorrow never comes just as we feared it would. Tomorrow is all right;

it carries in its grip good things as well as troubles. Bless my soul, when I sit down and think over the things which I once feared might possibly descend upon me, I laugh! Where are those feared things now? I don't know — have almost forgotten that I ever feared them.

You do not need fight Worry — that isn't the way to overcome the habit. Just practice concentration, and then learn to concentrate upon something right before you, and you will find that the worry thought has vanished. The mind can think of but one thing at a time, and if you concentrate upon a bright thing, the other thing will fade away. There are better ways of overcoming objectionable thoughts than by fighting them. Learn to concentrate upon thoughts of an opposite character, and you will have solved the problem.

When the mind is full of worry thoughts, it cannot find time to work out plans to benefit you. But when you have concentrated upon bright, helpful thoughts, you will discover that it will start to work subconsciously; and when the time comes you will find all sorts of plans and methods by which you will be able to meet the demands upon you. Keep your mental attitude right, and all things will be added unto you. There's no sense in worrying; nothing has ever been gained by it, and nothing ever will be. Bright, cheerful and happy thoughts attract bright, cheerful and happy things to us — worry drives them away. Cultivate the right mental attitude.

# The Law of Mental Control

Your thoughts are either faithful servants or tyrannical masters — just as you allow them to be. You have the say about it; take your choice. They will either go about your work under direction of the firm will, doing it the best they know how, not only in your waking hours, but when you are asleep — some of our best mental work being performed for us when our conscious mentality is at rest, as is evidenced by the fact that when the morning comes we find troublesome problems have been worked out for us during the night, after we had dismissed them from our minds — apparently; or they will ride all over us and make us their slaves if we are foolish enough to allow them to do so. More than half the people of the world are slaves of every vagrant thought which may see fit to torment them.

Your mind is given you for your good and for your own use — not to use you. There are very few people who seem to realize this and who understand the art of managing the mind. The key to the mystery is Concentration. A little practice will develop within every man the power to use the mental machine properly. When you have some mental work to do concentrate upon it to the exclusion of everything else, and you will find that the mind will get right down to business — to the work at hand — and matters will be cleared up in no time. There is an absence of friction, and all waste motion or lost power is obviated. Every pound of energy is put to use, and every revolution of the mental driving wheel counts for something. It pays to be able to be a competent mental engineer.

And the man who understands how to run his mental engine knows that one of the important things is to be able to stop it when the work has been done. He does not keep putting coal in the furnace, and maintaining a high pressure after the work is finished, or when the day's portion of the work has been done, and the fires should be banked until the next day. Some people act as if the engine should be kept running whether there was any work to be done or not, and then they complain if it gets worn out and wobbles and needs repairing. These mental engines are fine machines, and need intelligent care.

To those who are acquainted with the laws of mental control it seems absurd for one to lie awake at night fretting about the problems of the day, or more often, of the morrow. It is just as easy to slow down the mind as it is to slow down an engine, and thousands of people are learning to do this in these days of New Thought. The best way to do it is to think of something else — as far different from the obtruding thought as possible. There is no use fighting an objectionable thought with the purpose of "downing" it — that is a great waste of energy, and the more you keep on saying, "I won't think of this thing!" the more it keeps on coming into your mind, for you are holding it there for the purpose of hitting it. Let it go; don't give it another thought; fix the mind on something entirely different, and keep the attention there by an effort of the will. A little practice will do much for you in this direction. There is only room for one thing at a time in the focus of attention; so put all your attention upon one thought, and the others will sneak off. Try it for yourself.

## Asserting the Life-Force

I have spoken to you of the advantage of getting rid of Fear. Now I wish to put *life* into you. Many of you have been going along as if you were dead — no ambition — no energy — no vitality — no interest — no life. This will never do. You are stagnating. Wake up and display a few signs of life! This is not the place in which you can stalk around like a living corpse — this is the place for wide—awake, active, live people, and a good general awakening is what is needed; although it would take nothing less than a blast from Gabriel's trumpet to awaken some of the people who are stalking around thinking that they are alive, but who are really dead to all that makes life worthwhile.

We must let Life flow through us, and allow it to express itself naturally. Do not let the little worries of life, or the big ones either, depress you and cause you to lose your vitality. Assert the Life Force within you, and manifest it in every thought, act and deed, and before long you will be exhilarated and fairly bubbling over with vitality and energy.

Put a little life into your work — into your pleasures — into yourself. Stop doing things in a half-headed way, and begin to take an interest in what you are doing, saying and thinking. It is astonishing how much interest we may find in the ordinary things of life if we will only wake up. There are interesting things all around us — interesting events occurring every moment — but we will not be aware of them unless we assert our life force and begin to actually live instead of merely existing.

No man or woman ever amounted to anything unless he or she put life into the tasks of everyday life — the acts — the thoughts. What the world needs is live men and women. Just look into the eyes of the people whom you meet, and see how few of them are really alive. The most of them lack that expression of conscious life which distinguishes the man who lives from the one who simply exists.

I want you to acquire this sense of conscious life so that you may manifest it in your life and show what Mental Science has done for you. I want you to get to work today and begin to make yourselves over according to the latest pattern. You can do this if you will only take the proper interest in the task.

### Affirmation and Exercise

Fix in your mind the thought that the "I" within you is very much alive and that you are manifesting life fully, mentally and physically.

And keep this though there, aiding yourself with constant repetitions of the watchword. Don't let the thought escape you, but keep pushing it back into the mind. Keep it before the mental vision as much as possible. Repeat the watchword when you awaken in the morning — say it when you retire at night. And say it at meal times, and whenever else you can during the day — at least once an hour. Form the mental picture of yourself as filled with Life and Energy. Live up to it as far as possible. When you start in to perform a task say "I *Am* Alive" and mix up as much life as possible in the task. If you find yourself feeling depressed, say "I *Am* Alive," and then take a few deep breaths, and with each inhalation let the mind hold the thought that you are breathing in Strength and Life, and as you exhale, hold the thought that you are breathing out all the old, dead, negative conditions and are glad to get rid of them. Then finish up with an earnest, vigorous affirmation: "I *Am* Alive," and mean it when you say it too.

And let your thoughts take form in action. Don't rest content with merely saying that you are alive, but prove it with your acts. Take an interest in doing things, and don't go around "mooning" or daydreaming. Get down to business, and *Live*.

# Training the Habit-Mind

Professor William James, the well-known teacher of, and writer upon Psychology very truly says: "The great thing in all education is to make our nervous system our ally instead of our enemy. For this we must make automatic and habitual, as early as possible, as many useful actions as we can and as carefully guard against growing into ways that are likely to be disadvantageous. In the acquisition of a new habit, or the leaving off of an old one we must take care to launch ourselves with as strong and decided initiative as possible. Never suffer an exception to occur until the new habit is securely rooted in your life. Seize the very first possible opportunity to act on every resolution you make and on every emotional prompting you may experience, in the direction of the habits you aspire to gain."

This advice is along the lines familiar to all students of Mental Science, but it states the matter more plainly than the majority of us have done. It impresses upon us the importance of passing on to the subconscious mind the proper impulses, so that they will become automatic and "second nature." Our subconscious mentality is a great storehouse for all sorts of suggestions from ourselves and others and, as it is the "habit-mind," we must be careful to send it the proper material from which it may make habits. If we get into the habit of doing certain things, we may be sure that the subconscious mentality will make it easier for us to do just the same thing over and over again, easier each time, until finally we are firmly bound with the ropes and chains of the habit, and find it more or less difficult, sometimes almost impossible, to free ourselves from the hateful thing.

We should cultivate good habits against the hour of need. The time will come when we will be required to put forth our best efforts, and it rests with us today whether that hour of need shall find us doing the proper thing automatically and almost without thought, or struggling to do it bound down and hindered with the chains of things opposed to that which we desire at that moment.

We must be on guard at all times to prevent the forming of undesirable habits. There may be no special harm in doing a certain thing today, or perhaps again tomorrow, but there may be much harm in setting up the habit of of doing that particular thing. If you are confronted with the question: "Which of these two things should I do?"

the best answer is: "I will do that which I would like to become a habit with me."

In forming a new habit, or in breaking an old one, we should throw ourselves into the task with as much enthusiasm as possible, in order to gain the most ground before the energy expends itself when it meets with friction from the opposing habits already formed. We should start in by making as strong an impression as possible upon the subconscious mentality. Then we should be constantly on guard against temptations to break the new resolution "just this once." This "just once" idea kills off more good resolutions than any other one cause. The moment you yield "just this once, you introduce the thin edge of the wedge that will, in the end, split your resolution into pieces.

Equally important is the fact that each time you resist temptation the stronger does your resolution become. Act upon your resolution as early and as often as possible, as with every manifestation of thought in action, the stronger does it become. You are adding to the strength of your original resolution every time you back it up with action.

The mind has been likened to a piece of paper that has been folded. Ever afterwards it has a tendency to fold in the same crease — unless we make a new crease or fold, when it will follow the last lines. And the creases are habits — every time we make one it is so much easier for the mind to fold along the same crease afterward. Let us make our mental creases in the right direction.

# The Psychology of Emotion

One is apt to think of the emotions as independent from habit. We easily may think of one acquiring habits of action, and even of thinking, but we are apt to regard the emotions as something connected with "feeling" and quite divorced from intellectual effort. Yet, not withstanding the distinction between the two, both are dependent largely upon habit, and one may repress, increase, develop, and change one's emotions, just as one may regulate habits of action and lines of thought.

It is an axiom of psychology that "Emotions deepen by repetition." If a person allows a state of feeling to thoroughly take possession of him, he will find it easier to yield to the same emotion the second time, and so on, until the particular emotion or feeling becomes second nature to him. If an undesirable emotion shows itself inclined to take up a permanent abode with you, you had better start to work to get rid of it, or at least to master it. And the best time to do this is at the start; for each repetition renders the habit more firmly entrenched, and the task of dislodging it more difficult.

Were you ever jealous? If so, you will remember how insidious was its first approach; how subtly it whispered hateful suggestions into your willing ear, and how gradually it followed up such suggestions, until, finally you began to see green. (Jealousy has an effect upon the bile, and causes it to poison the blood. This is why the idea of green is always associated with it.) Then you will remember how the thing seemed to grow, taking possession of you until you scarcely could shake it off. You found it much easier to become jealous the next time. It seemed to bring before you all sorts of objects apparently justifying your suspicions and feeling. Everything began to look green — the green-eyed monster waxed fat.

And so it is with every feeling or emotion. If you give way to a fit of rage, you will find it easier to become angry the next time, on less provocation. The habit of feeling and acting "mean" does not take long to firmly settle itself in its new home if encouraged. Worry is a great habit for growing and waxing fat. People start by worrying about big things, and then begin to worry and fret about some smaller thing. And then the merest trifle worries and distresses them. They imagine that all sorts of evil things are about to befall them. If they start on a journey they are certain there is going to be a wreck. If a telegram comes, it is sure to contain some dreadful tidings. If a child seems a little quiet, the worrying mother is positive it is going to fall ill and die. If the husband seems thoughtful, as he revolves some business plan in his mind, then the good wife is convinced that he is beginning to cease to love her, and indulges in a crying spell. And so it goes — worry, worry, worry — each indulgence making the habit more at home. After a while the continued thought shows itself in action. Not only is the mind poisoned by the blue thoughts, but the forehead shows deep lines between the eyebrows, and the voice takes on that whining, rasping tone so common among worry-burdened people.

The condition of mind known as "fault-finding" is another emotion that grows fat with exercise. First, fault is found with this thing, then with that, and finally with everything. The person becomes a chronic "nagger" — a burden to friends and relatives, and a thing to be avoided by outsiders. Women make the greatest naggers. Not because men are any better, but simply because a man nagger apt to have the habit knocked out of him by other men who will not stand his nonsense — he find that he is making things too hot for himself and he reforms; while a woman has more of a chance to indulge in the habit. But this nagging is all a matter of habit. It grows from small beginnings, and each time it is indulged in it throws out another root, branch, or tendril, and fastens itself the closer to the one who has given it soil in which to grow.

Envy, uncharitableness, gossip scandal-mongering, are all habits of this kind. The seeds are in every human breast, and only need good soil and a little watering to become lusty and strong.

Each time you give way to one of these negative emotions, the easier do you make it for a recurrence of the same thing, or similar ones. Sometimes by encouraging one unworthy emotion, you find that you have given room for the growth of a whole family of these mental weeds.

Now, this is not a good old orthodox preachment against the sin of bad thoughts. It is merely a calling of your attention to the law underlying the psychology of emotion. Nothing new about it — old as the hills — so old that many of us have forgotten all about it.

If you wish to manifest these constantly disagreeable and unpleasant traits, and to suffer the unhappiness that comes from them, by all means do so — that is your own business, and privilege. It's none of mine, and I am not preaching at you — it keeps me busy minding my own business and keeping an eye on my own undesirable habits and actions. I am merely telling you the law regarding the matter, and you may do the rest. If you wish to choke out these habits, there are two ways open to you. First, whenever you find yourself indulging in a negative thought or feeling, take right hold of it and say to it firmly, and vigorously, "Get out!" It won't like this at first, and will bridle up, curve its back and snarl like an offended cat. But never mind — just say, "Scat" to it. The next time it will not be so confident and aggressive — it will have manifested a little of the fear-habit. Each time you repress and choke out a tendency of this kind, the weaker it will become, and the stronger will your will be.

Professor James says: "Refuse to express a passion, and it dies. Count ten before venting your anger, and its occasion seems ridiculous. Whistling to keep up courage is no mere figure of speech. On the other hand, sit all day in a moping posture, sigh, and reply to everything with a dismal voice, and your melancholy lingers. There is no more valuable precept in moral education than this, as all who have experience know: if we wish to conquer emotional tendencies in ourselves, we must assiduously, and in the first instance, cold-bloodedly, go through the outward movements of those contrary dispositions we prefer to cultivate.

Smooth the brow, brighten the eye, contract the dorsal rather than the ventral aspect of the frame, and speak in a major key, pass the genial compliment, and your heart must be frigid indeed if it does not gradually thaw.

# Developing New Brain Cells

I have spoken of the plan of getting rid of undesirable states of feeling by driving them out. But a far better way is to cultivate the feeling or emotion directly opposed to the one you wish to eradicate.

We are very apt to regard ourselves as the creatures of our emotions and feelings, and to fancy that these feelings and emotions are "we." But such is far from being the truth. It is true that the majority of the race are slaves of their emotions and feelings, and are governed by them to a great degree. They think that feelings are things that rule one and from which one cannot free himself, and so they cease to rebel. They yield to the feeling without question, although they may know that the emotion or mental trait is calculated to injure them, and to bring unhappiness and failure instead of happiness and success. They say, "We are made that way," and let it go at that.

The new Psychology is teaching the people better things. It tells them that they are masters of their emotions and feelings, instead of being their slaves. It tells them that brain-cells may be developed that will manifest along desirable lines, and that the old brain-cells that have been manifesting so unpleasantly may be placed on the retired list, and allowed to atrophy from want of use. People may make themselves over, and change their entire natures. This is not mere idle theory, but is a working fact which has been demonstrated by thousands of people, and which is coming more and more before the attention of the race.

No matter what theory of mind we entertain, we must admit that the brain is the organ and instrument of the mind, in our present state of existence, at least, and that the brain must be considered in this matter. The brain is like a wonderful musical instrument, having millions of keys, upon which we may play innumerable combinations of sounds. We come into the world with certain tendencies, temperaments, and predispositions, We may account for these tendencies by heredity, or we may account for them upon theories of preexistence, but the facts remain the same. Certain keys seem to respond to our touch more easily than others. Certain notes seem to sound forth as the current of circumstances sweeps over the strings. And certain other notes are less easily vibrated. But we find that if we but make an effort of the will to restrain the utterance of some of these easily sounded strings, they will grow more difficult to sound, and less

liable to be stirred by the passing breeze. And if we will pay attention
to some of the other strings that have not been giving forth a clear tone,
we will soon get them in good working order; their notes will chime
forth clear and vibrant, and will drown the less pleasant sounds.

We have millions of unused brain-cells awaiting our cultivation. We
are using but a few of them, and some of these we are working to
death. We are able to give some of these cells a rest, by using other
cells. The brain may be trained and cultivated in a manner incredible
to one who has not looked into the subject. Mental attitudes may be
acquired and cultivated, changed and discarded, at will. There is no
longer any excuse for people manifesting unpleasant and harmful
mental states. We have the remedy in our own hands.

We acquire habits of thought, feeling, and action, repeated use. We
may be born with a tendency in a certain direction, or we may acquire
tendencies by suggestions from other; such as the examples of those
around us, suggestions from reading, listening to teachers. We are a
bundle of mental habits. Each time we indulge in an undesirable
thought or habit, the easier does it become for us to repeat that thought
or action.

Mental scientists are in the habit of speaking of desirable thoughts
or mental attitudes as "positive," and of the undesirable ones as
"negative." There is a good reason for this. The mind instinctively
recognizes certain things as good for the individual to which it belongs,
and it clears the path for such thoughts, and interposes the least
resistance to them. They have a much greater effect than an
undesirable thought possesses, and one positive thought will
counteract a number of negative thoughts. The best way to overcome
undesirable or negative thoughts and feelings is to cultivate the
positive ones. The positive thought is the strongest plant, and will in
time starve out the negative one by withdrawing from it the
nourishment necessary for its existence.

Of course the negative thought will set up a vigorous resistance at
first, for it is a fight for life with it. In the slang words of the time, it
"sees its finish" if the positive thought is allowed to grow and develop;
and, consequently it makes things unpleasant for the individual until
he has started well into the work of starving it out. Brain cells do not
like to be laid on the shelf any more than does any other form of living
energy, and they rebel and struggle until they become too weak to do
so. The best way is to pay as little attention as possible to these weeds
of the mind, but put in as much time as possible watering, caring for
and attending to the new and beautiful plants in the garden of the
mind.

For instance, if you are apt to hate people, you can best overcome the negative thought by cultivating Love in its place. Think Love, and act it out, as often as possible. Cultivate thoughts of kindness, and act as kindly as you can to everyone with whom you come in contact. You will have trouble at the start, but gradually Love will master Hate, and the latter will begin to droop and wither. If you have a tendency toward the "blues" cultivate a smile, and a cheerful view of things. Insist upon your mouth wearing upturned corners, and make an effort of the will to look upon the bright side of things. The "blue-devils" will set up a fight, of course, but pay no attention to them — just go on cultivating optimism and cheerfulness. Let "Bright, Cheerful and Happy" be your watchword, and try to live it out.

These recipes may seem very old and timeworn, but they are psychological truths and may be used by you to advantage. If you once comprehend the nature of the thing, the affirmations and autosuggestions of the several schools may be understood and taken advantage of. You may make yourself energetic instead of slothful, active instead of lazy, by this method. It is all a matter of practice and steady work. New Thought people often have much to say about "holding the thought;" and, indeed, it is necessary to "hold the thought" in order to accomplish results. But something more is needed. You must "act out" the thought until it becomes a fixed habit with you. Thoughts take form in action; and in turn actions influence thought. So by "acting out" certain lines of thought, the actions react upon the mind, and increase the development of the part of the mind having close relation to the act. Each time the mind entertains a thought, the easier becomes the resulting action — and each time an act is performed, the easier becomes the corresponding thought. So you see the thing works both ways — action and reaction. If you feel cheerful and happy, it is very natural for you to laugh. And if you will laugh a little, you will begin to feel bright and cheerful. Do you see what I am trying to get at? Here it is, in a nutshell: if you wish to cultivate a certain habit of action, begin by cultivating the mental attitude corresponding to it. And as a means of cultivating that mental attitude, start in to "act-out " or go through, the motions of the act corresponding to the thought. Now, see if you cannot apply this rule. Take up something that you really feel should be done, but which you do not feel like doing. Cultivate the thought leading up to it — say to yourself: "I like to do so and so," and then go through the motions (cheerfully, remember!) and act out the thought that you like to do the thing. Take an interest in the doing — study out the best way to do it — put brains into it — take a pride in it — and you will find yourself doing the thing with a considerable amount of pleasure and interest — you will have cultivated a new habit.

If you prefer trying it on some mental trait of which you wish to be rid, it will work the same way. Start in to cultivate the opposite trait, and think it out and act it out for all you are worth. Then watch the change that will come over you. Don't be discouraged at the resistance you will encounter at first, but sing gaily: "I Can and I Will," and get to work in earnest. The important thing in this work is to keep cheerful and interested. If you manage to do this, the rest will be easy.

# The Attractive Power — Desire Force

We have discussed the necessity of getting rid of fear, that your desire may have full strength with which to work. Supposing that you have mastered this part of the task, or at least started on the road to mastery, I will now call your attention to another important branch of the subject. I allude to the subject of mental leaks. No, I don't mean the leakage arising from your failure to keep your own secrets — that is also important, but forms another story. The leakage I am now referring to is that occasioned by the habit of having the attention attracted to and distracted by every passing fancy.

In order to attain a thing it is necessary that the mind should fall in love with it, and be conscious of its existence, almost to the exclusion of everything else. You must get in love with the thing you wish to attain, just as much as you would if you were to meet the girl or man you wished to marry. I do not mean that you should become a monomaniac upon the subject, and should lose all interest in everything else in the world — that won't do, for the mind must have recreation and change. But, I do mean that you must be so "set" upon the desired thing that all else will seem of secondary importance. A man in love may be pleasant to everyone else, and may go through the duties and pleasures of life with good spirit, but underneath it all he is humming to himself "Just One Girl," and every one of his actions is bent toward getting that girl, and making a comfortable home for her. Do you see what I mean? You must get in love with the thing you want, and you must get in love with it in earnest — none of this latter-day flirting, "on-today and off-tomorrow" sort of love, but the good old-fashioned kind, that used to make it impossible for a young man to get to sleep unless he took a walk around his best girl's house, just to be sure it was still there. That's the real kind!

And the man or woman in search of success must make of that desired thing his ruling passion — he must keep his mind on the main chance. Success is jealous — that's why we speak of her as feminine. She demands a man's whole affection, and if he begins flirting with other fair charmers, she soon turns her back upon him. If a man allows his strong interest in the main chance to be sidetracked, he will be the loser. Mental Force operates best when it is concentrated. You must give to the desired thing your best and most earnest thought. Just as the man who is thoroughly in love will think out plans and schemes whereby he may please the fair one, so will the man who is in love with his work or business give it his best thought, and the result will be that a hundred and one plans will come into his field of consciousness, many of which are very important. The mind works on the subconscious plane, remember, and almost always along the lines of the ruling passion or desire. It will fix up things, and patch together plans and schemes, and when you need them the most it will pop them into your consciousness, and you will feel like hurrahing, just as if you had received some valuable aid from outside.

But if you scatter your thought-force, the subconscious mind will not know just how to please you, and the result is that you are apt to be put off from this source of aid and assistance. Beside this, you will miss the powerful result of concentrated thought in the conscious working out of the details of your plans. And then again the man whose mind is full of a dozen interests fails to exert the attracting power that is manifested by the man of the one ruling passion, and he fails to draw to him persons, things, and results that will aid in the working out of his plans, and will also fail to place himself in the current of attraction whereby he is brought into contact with those who will be glad to help him because of harmonious interests.

I have noticed, in my own affairs, that when I would allow myself to be side-tracked by anything outside of my regular line of work, it would be only a short time before my receipts dropped off, and my business showed signs of a lack of vitality. Now, many may say that this was because I left undone some things that I would have done if my mind had been centered on the business. This is true; but I have noticed like results in cases where there was nothing to be done — cases in which the seed was sown, and the crop was awaited. And in just such cases, as soon as I directed my thought to the matter the seed began to sprout. I do not man that I had to send out great mental waves with the idea of affecting people — not a bit of it. I simply began to realize what a good thing I had, and how much people wanted it, and how glad they would be to know of it and all that sort of thing, and lo! My thought seemed to vitalize the work, and the seed began to sprout. This is no mere fancy, for I have experienced it on several occasions; I have spoken to many others on the subject, and I find that our experiences tally perfectly. So don't get into the habit of permitting these mental leaks. Keep your Desire fresh and active, and let it get in its work without interference from conflicting desires. Keep in love with the thing you wish to attain — feed your fancy with it — see it as accomplished already, but don't lose your interest. Keep your eye on the main chance, and keep your one ruling passion strong and vigorous.

Don't be a mental polygamist — one mental love is all that a man needs — that is, one at a time.

Some scientists have claimed that something that might as well be called "Love" is at the bottom of the whole of life. They claim that the love of the plant for water causes it to send forth its roots until the loved thing is found. They say that the love of the flower for the sun causes it to grow away from the dark places, so that it may receive the light. The so called "chemical affinities" are really a form of love. And Desire is a manifestation of this Universal Life Love. So I am not using a mere figure of speech when I tell you that you must love the thing you wish to attain. Nothing but intense love will enable you to surmount the many obstacles placed in your path. Nothing but that love will enable you to bear the burdens of the task. The more Desire you have for a thing, the more you Love it; and the more you Love it, the greater will be the attractive force exerted toward its attainment — both within yourself, and outside of you.

So love but one thing at a time — don't be a mental Mormon.

# The Great Dynamic Forces

You have noticed the difference between the successful and strong men in any walk of life, and the unsuccessful weak men around them. You are conscious of the widely differing characteristics of the two classes, but somehow find it difficult to express just in what the difference lies. Let us take a look at the matter.

Burton said: "The longer I live, the more certain I am that the great difference between men, the feeble and the powerful, the great and the insignificant, is energy and invincible determination — a purpose once fixed and then Death or Victory. That quality will do anything that can be done in this world — and no talents, no circumstances, no opportunities will make a two-legged creature a man without it." I do not see how the idea could be more clearly expressed than Burton has spoken. He has put his finger right in the center of the subject — his eye has seen into the heart of it.

Energy and invincible determination — these two things will sweep away mighty barriers, and will surmount the greatest obstacles. And yet they must be used together. Energy without determination will go to waste. Lots of men have plenty of energy — they are full to overflowing with it; and yet they lack concentration — they lack the concentrated force that enables them to bring their power to bear upon the right spot. Energy is not nearly so rare a thing as many imagine it to be. I can look around me at any lime, and pick out a number of people I know who are full of energy — many of them are energy plus — and yet, somehow, they do not seem to make any headway. They are wasting their energy all the time. Now they are fooling with this thing — now meddling with that. They will take up some trifling thing of no real interest or importance, and waste enough energy and nervous force to carry them through a hard day's work, and yet when they are through, nothing has been accomplished.

Others who have plenty of energy, fail to direct it by the power of the Will toward the desired end. "Invincible determination" — those are the words. Do they not thrill you with their power? If you have something to do, get to work and do it. Marshal your energy, and then guide and direct it by your Will — bestow upon it that "invincible determination" and you will do the thing.

Everyone has within him a giant will, but the majority of us are too lazy to use it. We cannot get ourselves nerved up to the point at which we can say, truthfully: "I Will. If we can but pluck up our courage to that point, and will then pin it in place so that it will not slip back, we will be able to call into play that wonderful power — the Human Will. Man, as a rule, has but the faintest conception of the power of the Will, but those who have studied along the occult teachings, know that the Will is one of the great dynamic forces of the universe, and if harnessed and directed properly it is capable of accomplishing almost miraculous things.

"Energy and Invincible Determination: — aren't they magnificent words? Commit them to memory — press them like a die into the wax of your mind, and they will be a constant inspiration to you in hours of need. If you can get these words to vibrating in your being, you will be a giant among pygmies. Say these words over and over again, and see how you are filled with new life — see how your blood will circulate — how your nerves will tingle. Make these words a part of yourself, and then go forth anew to the battle of life, encouraged and strengthened. Put them into practice. "Energy and Invincible Determination" — let that be your motto in your work-a-day life, and you will be one of those rare men who are able to "do things."

Many persons are deterred from doing their best by the fact that they underrate themselves by comparison with the successful ones of life, or rather, overrate the successful ones by comparison with themselves.

One of the curious things noticed by those who are brought in contact with the people who have "arrived" is the fact that these successful people are not extraordinary after all. You meet with some great writer, and you are disappointed to find him very ordinary indeed. He does not converse brilliantly, and, in fact, you know a score of everyday people who seem far more brilliant than this man who dazzles you by his brightness in his books. You meet some great statesman, and he does not seem nearly so wise as lots of old fellows in your own village, who waste their wisdom upon the desert air. You meet some great captain of industry, and he does not give you the impression of the shrewdness so marked in some little bargain-driving trader in your own town. How is this, anyway? Are the reputations of these people fictitious, or what is the trouble

The trouble is this: you have imagined these people to be made of superior metal, and are disappointed to find them made of the same stuff as yourself and those about you. But, you ask, wherein does their greatness of achievement lie? Chiefly in this: Belief in themselves and in their inherent power, in their faculty to concentrate on the work in hand, when they are working, and in their ability to prevent leaks of power when they are not working. They believe in themselves, and make every effort count. Your village wise man spills his wisdom on every corner, and talks to a lot of fools; when if he really were wise he would save up his wisdom and place it where it would do some work. The brilliant writer does not waste his wit upon every corner; in fact, he shuts the drawer in which he contains his wit, and opens it only when he is ready to concentrate and get down to business. The captain of industry has no desire to impress you with his shrewdness and "smartness. He never did, even when he was young. While his companions were talking and boasting, and "blowing," this future successful financier was "sawin' wood and sayin' nuthin'."

The great people of the world — that is, those who have "arrived" — are not very different from you, or me, or the rest of us — all of us are about the same at the base. You have only to meet them to see how very "ordinary" they are, after all. But, don't forget the fact that they know how to use the material that is in them; while the rest of the crowd does not, and, in fact, even doubts whether the true stuff is there. The man or woman who "gets there", usually starts out by realizing that he or she is not so very different, after all, from the successful people that they hear so much about. This gives them confidence, and the result is they find out that they are able to "do things." Then they learn to keep their mouths closed, and to avoid wasting and dissipating their energy. They store up energy, and concentrate it upon the task at hand; while their companions are scattering their energies in every direction, trying to show off and let people know how smart they are. The man or woman who "gets there," prefers to wait for the applause that follows deed accomplished, and cares very little for the praise that attends promises of what we expect to do "some day," or an exhibition of "smartness" without works.

One of the reasons that people who are thrown in with successful men often manifest success themselves, is that they are able to watch the successful man and sort of "catch the trick" of his greatness. They see that he is an everyday sort of man, but that he thoroughly believes in himself, and also that he does not waste energy, but reserves all his force for the actual tasks before him. And, profiting by example, they start to work and put the lesson into practice in their own lives.

Now what is the moral of this talk? Simply this: Don't undervalue yourself, or overvalue others. Realize that you are made of good stuff, and that locked within your mind are many good things. Then get to work and unfold those good things, and make something out of that good stuff. Do this by attention to the things before you, and by giving to each the best that is in you, knowing that plenty of more good things are in you ready for the fresh tasks that will come. Put the best of yourself into the undertaking on hand, and do not cheat the present task in favor of some future one. Your supply is inexhaustible. And don't waste your good stuff on the crowd of gapers, watchers and critics who are standing around watching you work. Save your good stuff for your job, and don't be in too much of a hurry for applause. Save up your good thoughts for "copy" if you are a writer; save up your bright schemes for actual practice, if you are a business man; save up your wisdom for occasion, if you are a statesman; and, in each case, avoid the desire to scatter your pears before — well, before the gaping crowd that wants to be entertained by a "free show."

Nothing very "high" about this teaching, perhaps, but it is what many of you need very much. Stop fooling, and get down to business. Stop wasting good raw material, and start to work making something worthwhile.

# Claiming Your Own

In a recent conversation, I was telling a woman to pluck up courage and to reach out for a certain good thing for which she had been longing for many years, and which, at last, appeared to be in sight. I told her that it looked as if her desire was about to be gratified — that the Law of Attraction was bringing it to her. She lacked faith, and kept on repeating, "Oh! It's too good to be true — it's too good for me! She had not emerged from the worm-of-the-dust stage, and although she was in sight of the Promised Land she refused to enter it because it "was too good for her." I think I succeeded in putting sufficient "ginger" into her to enable her to claim her own, for the last reports indicate that she is taking possession.

But that is not what I wish to tell you. I want to call your attention to the fact that nothing is too good for *you* — no matter how great the thing may be — no matter how undeserving you may seem to be. You are entitled to the best there is, for it is your direct inheritance. So don't be afraid to ask — demand — and take. The good things of the world are not the portion of any favored sons. They belong to all, but they come only to those who are wise enough to recognize that the good things are theirs by right, and who are sufficiently courageous to reach out for them. Many good things are lost for want of the asking. Many splendid things are lost to you because of your feeling that you are unworthy of them. Many great things are lost to you because you lack the confidence and courage to demand and take possession of them.

"None but the brave deserves the fair," says the old adage, and the rule is true in all lines of human effort. If you keep on repeating that you are unworthy of the good thing — that it is too good for you — the Law will be apt to take you at your word and believe what you say. That's a peculiar thing about the Law — it believes — what you say — it takes you in earnest. So beware what you say to it, for it will be apt to give credence. Say to it that you are worthy of the best there is, and that there is nothing too good for you, and you will be likely to have the Law take you in earnest, and say, "I guess he is right; I'm going to give him the whole bakeshop if he wants it — he knows his rights, and what's the use of trying to deny it to him?" But if you say, "Oh, it's too good for me! The Law will probably say, "Well, I wouldn't wonder but that that is so. Surely he ought to know, and it isn't for me to contradict him." And so it goes.

Why should anything be too good for you? Did you ever stop to think just what you are? You are a manifestation of the Whole Thing, and have a perfect right to all there is. Or, if you prefer it this way, you are a child of the Infinite, and are heir to it all. You are telling the truth in either statement, or both. At any rate, no matter for what you ask, you are merely demanding your own. And the more in earnest you are about demanding it — the more confident you are of receiving it — the more will you use in reaching out for it — the surer you will be to obtain it.

Strong desire — confident expectation — courage in action — these things bring to you your own. But before you put these forces into effect, you must awaken to a realization that you are merely asking for your own, and not for something to which you have no right or claim. So long as there exists in your mind the last sneaking bit of doubt as to your right to the things you want, you will be setting up a resistance to the operation of the Law. You may demand as vigorously as you please, but you will lack the courage to act, if you have a lingering doubt of your right to the thing you want. If you persist in regarding the desired thing as if it belonged to another, instead of to yourself, you will be placing yourself in the position of the covetous or envious man, or even in the position of a tempted thief. In such a case your mind will revolt at proceeding with the work, for it instinctively will recoil from the idea of taking what is not your own — the mind is honest. But when your realize that the best the Universe holds belongs to you as a Divine Heir, and that there is enough for all without your robbing anyone else; then the friction is removed, and the barrier broken down, and the Law proceeds to do its work.

I do not believe in this "humble" business. This meek and lowly attitude does not appeal to me — there is no sense in it, at all. The idea of making a virtue of such things, when Man is the heir of the Universe, and is entitled to whatever he needs for his growth, happiness and satisfaction! I do not mean that one should assume a blustering and domineering attitude of mind — that is also absurd, for true strength does not so exhibit itself. The blusterer is a self-confessed weakling — he blusters to disguise his weakness. The truly strong man is calm, self-contained, and carries with him a consciousness of strength which renders unnecessary the bluster and fuss of assumed strength. But get away from this hypnotism of "humility" — this "meek and lowly" attitude of mind. Remember the horrible example of Uriah Heep, and beware of imitating him. Throw back you head, and look the world square in the face. There's nothing to be afraid of — the world is apt to be as much afraid of you, as yell are of it, anyway. Be a man, or woman, and not a crawling thing. And this applies to your mental attitude, as well as to your outward demeanor. Stop this crawling in your mind. See yourself as standing erect and facing life without fear, and you will gradually grow into your ideal.

There is nothing that is too good for you — not a thing. The best there is, is not beginning to be good enough for you; for there are still better things ahead. The best gift that the world has to offer is a mere bauble compared to the great things in the Cosmos that await your coming of age. So don't be afraid to reach out for these playthings of life — these baubles of this plane of consciousness. Reach out for them — grab a whole fistful — play with them until you are tired; that's what they are made for, anyway. They are made for our express use — not to look at, but to be played with, if you desire. Help yourself — there's a whole shopful of these toys awaiting your desire, demand and taking. Don't be bashful! Don't let me hear any more of this silly talk about things being too good for you. Pshaw! You have been like the Emperor's little son thinking that the tin soldiers and toy drum were far too good for him, and refusing to reach out for them. But you don't find this trouble with children as a rule. They instinctively recognize that nothing is too good for them. They want all that is in sight to play with, and they seem to feel that the things are theirs by right. And that is the condition of mind that we seekers after the Divine Adventure must cultivate. Unless we become as little children we cannot enter the Kingdom of Heaven.

The things we see around us are the playthings of the Kindergarten of God, playthings which we use in our game-tasks. Help yourself to them — ask for them without bashfulness demand as many as you can make use of — they are yours. And if you don't see just what you want, ask for it — there's a big reserve stock on the shelves, and in the closets. Play, play, play, to your heart's content. Learn to weave mats — to build houses with the blocks — to stitch outlines on the squares — play the game through, and play it well. And demand all the proper materials for the play — don't be bashful — there's enough to go round.

But — remember this! While all this be true, the best things are still only game-things — toys, blocks, mats, cubes, and all the rest. Useful, most useful for the learning of the lessons — pleasant, most pleasant with which to play — and desirable, most desirable, for these purposes. Get all the fun and profit out of the use of things that is possible. Throw yourself heartily into the game, and play it out — it is Good. But, here's the thing to remember — never lose sight of the fact that these good things are but playthings — part of the game — and you must be perfectly willing to lay them aside when the time comes to pass into the next class, and not cry and mourn because you must leave your playthings behind you. Do not allow yourself to become unduly attached to them — they are for your use and pleasure, but are not a part of you — not essential to your happiness in the next stage. Despise them not because of their lack of Reality — they are great things relatively, and you may as well have all the fun out of them that you can — don't be a spiritual prig, standing aside and refusing to join in the game. But do not tie yourself to them — they are good to use and play with, but not good enough to use you and to make you a plaything. Don't let the toys turn the tables on you.

This is the difference between the master of Circumstances and the Slave of Circumstances. The Slave thinks that these playthings are real, and that he is not good enough to have them. He gets only a few toys, because he is afraid to ask for more, and he misses most of the fun. And then, considering the toys to be real, and not realizing that there are plenty more where these came from, he attaches himself to the little trinkets that have come his way, and allows himself to be made a slave of them. He is afraid that they may be taken away from him and he is afraid to toddle across the floor and help himself to the others. The Master knows that all are his for the asking. He demands that which he needs from day to day, and does not worry about over-loading himself; for he knows that there are "lots more," and that he cannot be cheated out of them. He plays, and plays well, and has a good time in the play — and he learns his Kindergarten lessons in the playing. But he does not become too much attached to his toys. He is willing to fling away the worn-out toys, and reach out for a new one. And when he is called into the next room for promotion, he drops on the floor the worn-out toys of the day, and with glistening eyes and confident attitude of mind, marches into the next room — into the Great Unknown — with a smile on his face. He is not afraid, for he hears the voice of the Teacher, and knows that she is there waiting for him — in that Great Next Room.

# Law, Not Chance

Some time ago I was talking to a man about the Attractive Power of Thought. He said that he did not believe that Thought could attract anything to him, and that it was all a matter of luck. He had found, he said, that ill luck relentlessly pursued him, and that everything he touched went wrong. It always had, and always would, and he had grown to expect it. When he undertook a new thing he knew beforehand that it would go wrong and that no good would come of it. Oh, no! There wasn't anything in the theory of Attractive Thought, so far as he could see; it was all a matter of luck!

This man failed to see that by his own confession he was giving a most convincing argument in favor of the Law of Attraction. He was testifying that he was always expecting things to go wrong, and that they always came about as he expected. He was a magnificent illustration of the Law of Attraction — but he didn't know it, and no argument seemed to make the matter clear to him. He was "up against it," and there was no way out of it — he always expected the ill luck. and every occurrence proved that he was right, and that the Mental Science position was all nonsense.

There are many people who seem to think that the only way in which the Law of Attraction operates is when one wishes hard, strong and steady. They do not seem to realize that a strong belief is as efficacious as a strong wish. The successful man believes in himself and his ultimate success, and, paying no attention to little setbacks, stumbles, tumbles and slips, presses on eagerly to the goal, believing all the time that he will get there. His views and aims may alter as he progresses, and he may change his plans or have them changed for him, but all the time he knows in his heart that he will eventually "get there." He is not steadily wishing he may get there — he simply feels and believes it, and thereby sets to operation the strongest forces known in the world of thought.

The man who just as steadily believes he is going to fail will invariably fail. How could he help it? There is no special miracle about it. Everything he does, thinks and says is tinctured with the thought of failure. Other people catch his spirit, and fail to trust him or his ability, which occurrences he in turn sets down as but other exhibitions of his ill luck, instead of ascribing them to his belief and expectation of failure. He is suggesting failure to himself all the time, and he invariably takes on the effect of the autosuggestion. Then, again, he by his negative thoughts shuts up that portion of his mind from which should come the ideas and plans conducive to success and which do come to the man who is expecting success because he believes in it. A state of discouragement is not the one in which bright ideas come to us. It is only when we are enthused and hopeful that our minds work out the bright ideas which we may turn to account.

Men instinctively feel the atmosphere of failure hovering around certain of their fellows, and on the other hand recognize something about others which leads them to say, when they hear of a temporary mishap befalling such a one: "Oh, he'll come out all right somehow — you can't down him." It is the atmosphere caused by the prevailing Mental Attitude. Clear up your Mental Atmosphere!

There is no such thing as chance. Law maintains everywhere, and all that happens  because of the operation of Law. You cannot name the simplest thing that ever occurred by chance — try it, and then run the thing down to a final analysis, and you will see it as the result of law. It is as plain as mathematics. Plan and purpose; cause and effect. From the movements of worlds to the growth of the grain of mustard seed — all the result of Law. The fall of the stone down the mountainside is not chance — forces which had been in operation for centuries caused it. And back of that cause were other causes, and so on until the Causeless Cause is reached.

And Life is not the result of chance — the Law is here, too. The Law is in full operation whether you know it or not — whether you believe in it or not. You may be the ignorant object upon      which the Law operates, and bring yourself all sorts of trouble because of your ignorance of or opposition to the Law. Or you may fall in with the operations to the Law — get into its current, as it were — and Life will seem a far different thing to you. You cannot get outside of the Law,

 by refusing to have anything to do with it. You are at liberty to oppose it and produce all the     friction you wish to — it doesn't' hurt the Law, and you may keep it up until you learn your lesson.

The Law of Thought Attraction is one name for the law, or rather for one manifestation of it. Again I say, your thoughts are real things. They go forth from you in all directions, combining with thoughts of like kind — opposing thoughts of a different character — forming combinations — going where they are attracted — flying away from thought centers opposing them. And your mind attracts the thought of others, which have been sent out by them conscious or unconsciously. But it attracts only those thoughts which are in harmony with its own. Like attracts like, and opposites repel opposites, in the world of thought.

If you set your mind to the keynote of courage, confidence, strength and success, you attract to yourself thoughts of like nature; people of like nature; things that fit in the mental tune. Your prevailing thought or mood determines that which is to be drawn toward you — picks out your mental bedfellow. You are today setting into motion thought currents which will in time attract toward you thoughts, people and conditions in harmony with the predominant note of your thought. Your thought will mingle with that of others of like nature and mind, and you will be attracted toward each other, and will surely come together with a common purpose sooner or later, unless one or the other of you should change the current of his thoughts.

Fall in with the operations of the law. Make it a part of yourself. Get into its currents. Maintain your poise. Set your mind to the keynote of Courage, Confidence and Success. Get in touch with all the thoughts of that kind that are emanating every hour from hundreds of minds. Get the best that is to be had in the thought world. The best is there, so be satisfied with nothing less. Get into partnership with good minds. Get into the right vibrations. You must be tired of being tossed about by the operations of the Law — get into harmony with it.

# Practical Mental Influence

## A Course of Lessons on
Mental Vibrations, Psychic Influence, Personal Magnetism,
Fascination, Psychic Self-Protection, etc., etc.

## Containing
Practical Instruction, Exercises, Directions, etc.,
capable of being understood, mastered and demonstrated
by any person of average intelligence.

## Table of Contents

# THE LAW OF VIBRATION

Students of history find a continuous chain of reference to the mysterious influence of one human mind over that of others. In the earliest records, traditions and legends may be found giving reference to the general belief that it was possible for an individual to exert some weird uncanny power over the minds of other persons, which would influence the latter for good or evil. And more than this, the student will find an accompanying belief that certain individuals are possessed of some mental power which bends even "things" and circumstances to its might.

Way back in the dim past of man's history on this planet, this belief existed, and it has steadily persisted in spite of the strenuous opposition of material science, even unto the present day. The years have not affected the belief, and in these dawning days of the Twentieth Century it has taken on a new strength and vitality, for its adherents have boldly stepped to the front, and confronting the doubting materialistic thinkers, have claimed the name of "Science" for this truth and have insisted that it be taken, once and for all, from the category of superstition, credulity and ignorant phantasm.

Were it not pitiable, it would be amusing to glance at the presumptuous, complacent, smug, self-satisfied position of the materialistic school of thinkers, who would brush aside as a foolish delusion that which many of the wisest men of a past age have accepted and taught as the truth. The modern "know-it-alls" would sneer contemptuously at facts that are known to be of actual occurrence in the daily lives of thousands of intelligent people, and which the experience of humankind has demonstrated for many centuries, in all lands and all races.

The trouble lies in the dogmatic assumption of the materialistic school that what is known as "mind" is merely some peculiar action of the material brain, some writers even holding that "the brain secretes thought, just as the liver secretes bile." They refuse to see that the operation of Mind is a manifestation of energy known as electricity, magnetism, light, heat, gravitation, cohesion, etc. Because mental energy does not register the vibrations of these lower forms of energy, they conclude that the higher mental energy does not exist. Having formulated a theory to suit their materialistic conceptions, they try to ignore all facts not consistent with their theory. If they find a fact that will not squeeze into their narrow theory well, "so much the worse for the fact," as a writer has said and they promptly ignore or dispute it.

As a matter of truth, the investigator is not compelled to resort to metaphysical explanations to account for the phenomena of Mental Influence. The very facts of physical science itself, if rightly interpreted, will give the clue to the mystery; and will point the steps of the honest investigator toward the path where he may find the solution of the perplexing riddle. Although we know that the real solution lies in the metaphysical realm, still even physical science will corroborate the facts of its metaphysical sister science, and instead of contradicting the latter will actually go far toward furnishing analogous facts and principles basis for a theory of metaphysical facts.

The student will see at once that so far as physical science is concerned, it must begin at the phenomenon of "Thought Transference," for in that phase of the subject may be found an elementary principle in evidence in many other forms of phenomena. We have given many instances of "Thought Transference" in the two proceeding volumes of this series, entitled "Mind Reading" and "Psychomancy," respectively, and so we need not repeat the same in this place. The main fact is that "Thought Transference" does exist, and may be accounted for upon purely scientific grounds, without calling in the truths of metaphysical thought. We know that this is a strong statement, and a positive assertion, but we also know that the same may be demonstrated. Let us consider this phase of the subject.

In the first place, physical science teaches that underlying all forms, degrees and apparent differences in matter and energy, there is to be found a manifestation of some elementary energy, which manifests in what is known as "Vibrations." Everything in the material world is in vibration — ever manifesting a high degree of motion. Without vibration there would be no such thing as a material universe. From the electronic-corpuscles which science teaches compose the atom; up through the atom and molecule, until the most complex forms of matter are manifested, there is the ever-present Vibration. And through all forms of energy, light, heat, electricity, magnetism and the rest, Vibration is also ever present. In fact, physical science itself teaches that not only is Vibration the basic force underlying other forces and the various forms of matter, but also that the apparent differences between the various forms of matter, and also between the various forms of energy, are caused simply and solely by the varying degrees of Vibration manifested.

Just as the difference between the lowest tone that can be distinguished by the ear of man, and the highest note that can be distinguished by the same organ of sense, is merely a difference between the rate of Vibration — just as is the difference between the dull red color at one end of the spectrum, and the violet at the other end, with the intervening colors known as indigo, blue green, yellow and orange, with all the combinations of shades arising from them — just as the difference between the greatest degree of cold known to Science, and the greatest degree of heat that can be conceived of — just as these great differences due solely and wholly to varying rates of Vibration — so is the difference between and all forms of matter or force simply a matter of the rate of Vibration. In short, all material and physical "Things" are simply manifestations of some "infinite and eternal energy from which all things proceed," their differences resulting merely from the different degree of Vibration being manifested in them. Remember, that this is not "vague philosophy" or "airy metaphysics" or "spiritualistic vagaries" (to quote from the materialistic writers), but facts claimed and admitted by the greatest physical scientists of the age, as a reference to their lectures and textbooks will prove to anyone.

And, more than this, any intelligent physical scientist will tell you that Science has every reason to believe that there are great fields of energy and force, the Vibrations of which are far too high for even the delicate instruments of science to record, but which nevertheless exist and manifest effects. It was only the other day that Science was able to "catch" the "X-rays" and other forms of high Radioactivity, and yet these rays and forces had always existed. And tomorrow Science will perfect instruments capable of registering still higher forms of energy. And bye-and-bye, some scientist will perfect an instrument capable of registering and recording the subtle vibrations of Thought, and perhaps in time someone will perfect that instrument so that it will not only record such Thought vibrations and waves, but, like the phonograph, it will be able to reproduce and send forth similar vibrations so that others may feel the thoughts, just as they now hear the sounds from the phonograph. Such a prediction is no more wonderful then would have been the prediction of the telephone, the phonograph, the wireless telegraph and sundry other discoveries and inventions a hundred years ago.

Did you ever think that there are colors that the eye cannot see, but which delicate instruments clearly register? In fact, the rays of tight which sunburn the face, and which register on the photographic plate are not visible to the eye. The eye sees the lower rays, but only instruments adapted for the purpose detect the higher ones. Your eye cannot see the X-ray as it passes through the room, but the plate will catch it, and its light may make a photograph. The rays of light visible to the eyes are only the lower ones — the higher ones are far beyond the power of the eye to record, and beyond even the range of the most delicate instrument there exist rays and waves of light of such high vibratory rate as to defy even its power to record.

Did you ever know that there are sounds unheard by human ears that the microphone will catch and magnify? Scientific imagination dreams of instruments that will catch the songs of the mite — like insects, and magnify them until they can be distinguished. There are waves of electricity that may pass through your body, unperceived by you, and yet powerful enough to run light electric lights. Listen to the words of certain eminent scientists.

Prof. Elisha Gary, a celebrated scientist and teacher, has said: "There is much food for speculation in the thought that there exists sound waves that no human ear can hear, and color waves of light that no eye can see. The long, dark, soundless space between 40, 000 and 400,000,000,000,000 vibrations per second, and the infinity of range beyond 700,000,000,000,000 vibrations per second, where light ceases, in the universe of motion, makes it possible to indulge in speculation."

Prof. Williams, the well-known scientific writer, has said: "There is no gradation between the most rapid undulations or trembling that produces our sensations of sound, and the slowest of those which give rise to our sensations of gentlest warmth. There is a huge gap between them, wide enough to include another world of motion, all lying between our world of sound and our world of heat and light; and there is no good reason whatever for supposing that matter is incapable of such intermediate activity, or that such activity may not give rise to intermediate sensations, provided that there are organs for taking up and sensitizing their movements."

And, so you see that in the scientific theory of Vibrations, there may be found plenty of room for a scientific explanation of all that is claimed by adherents of the truth of Mental Influence, without getting out of the region of physical science, and without invading the plane of metaphysics. And there are many more proofs from the same source, which we may touch upon as we proceed.

There is but one Truth, and it manifests on all planes — the Spiritual; the Mental; and the Physical — and manifestations agree and coincide. So no Mentalist need fear the test of Physical Science, for each plane will bear out the facts and phenomena of the ones below or above it — the Three are but varying phases of One. In this little work we shall hug close to the plane of Physical Science, because by so doing we will be able to make the subject much clearer to many than if we had attempted to express the teaching in Metaphysical terms. There is no contradiction in the end. Each bit of Truth must dovetail into every other bit, for all are parts of the Whole.

# Thought Waves

In our last chapter we have seen that Vibration was to be found underlying all manifestations of energy, and all forms of matter. We also quoted two distinguished scientists whose words showed that there were fields of vibratory energy not filled by any known forms of energy, the inference being that inasmuch as there are no gaps in nature's processes these unknown fields must be occupied by certain forms of energy not known as yet to physical science. The teachings of the occultists of all lands and ages, as also those of modern Mental Science, are to the effect that the Mind, in its manifestation of Thought in the brain, generates a form of energy of intensely high Vibration, which energy may be, and is, projected in vibratory waves from the brains of other persons within its field of influence.

All students of Mental Influence have noticed the close resemblance that is manifested between the phenomena of electrical and magnetic energy on the one hand and the phenomena of mental energy on the other. So close is the analogy that one may take the proven facts of science relating to electrical and magnetic phenomena and confidently proceed with the certainty of finding a strikingly close correspondence in the field of mental phenomena. And the recognition of this fact is helping the workers in the mental field group together the varied phenomena that come under their notice, and to work out the theory and practice of Mental Influence.

In the first place, it is now a fact well known and accepted by investigators that the generation of Thought and the manifestation of Mental States occasions a "burning up" of brain matter, and the consequent production of a form of energy of high vibratory power. Physiologists recognize this fact, and the textbooks make reference to it. Experiments have shown that the temperature of the brain is increased in accordance with the intensity of Feeling and Thought, and that there is undoubtedly a generation of energy and a consumption of brain matter which bears a very close resemblance to the process of the generation of electrical energy. And this being conceded, it follows that this energy once released must be emanated or sent forth from the brain in the manner akin to the emanation of other known forms of energy, i.e., in the form of "waves" of vibratory force. Light and Heat travel in this way — so do electricity and magnetism — so do the forces of Radioactivity. And the investigators of Mental Influence have demonstrated by their experiments that there is such a thing as Thought-induction, and many other phases of manifestation similar to that exhibited by electricity and magnetism.

Flammarion, the well-known and eminent French scientist, has said on the subject. "We sum up, therefore, our preceding observations by the conclusion that one mind can act at a distance upon another, without the habitual medium of words, or any other visible means of communication. It appears to us altogether unreasonable to reject this conclusion if we accept the facts. The conclusion will be abundantly demonstrated. There is nothing unscientific, nothing romantic in admitting that an idea can influence a brain from a distance. The action of one human being upon another, from a distance, is a scientific fact, it is as certain as the existence of Paris, of Napoleon, of Oxygen, or of Sirius." The same authority also states: "There can be no doubt that our physical force creates a movement in the either which transmits itself afar like all movements in the ether, becomes perceptible to brains in harmony with our own. The transformation of a psychic action into an ethereal movement, and the reverse, may be analogous to what takes place on a telephone, where the receptive plate, which is identical with the plate at the other end, reconstructs the sonorous movement transmitted, not by means of sound, but by electricity. But these are only comparisons."

When a Thought or feeling is generated in the mind or brain of a person, the energy generated flows forth from the brain of the person in the form of waves of mental energy, spreading from the immediate neighborhood of the thinker to a distance proportioned to the strength of the thought or feeling. These Thought-Waves have the property of awakening similar vibrations in the minds of other persons coming within their field of force, according to the laws of Mental Influence, which law shall be explained in the next chapter.

As we proceed with our consideration of the subject of Mental Influence, in the succeeding chapters, we shall see the many and varied forms of manifestation of Thought-Waves. At this point we shall merely view the phenomena in a general way.

Thought-Waves are manifested in a variety of forms and phases. Some are the waves emanated from the minds of all thinkers, unconsciously and without purpose, and usually without much force. Others are sent forth with great force, and travel far, manifesting a degree of influence commensurate with the force with which they are projected. Others are directed purposely toward certain individuals or places, and travel along rapidly in a straight line to the point which they have been directed or aimed. Others are sent forth with great strength and power, but instead of being directed toward any particular person or place, are designed to sweep around in great whirlpools of energy affecting all who happen to fall within their field force.

You will readily understand that there is a great difference between Thought-Waves sent forth idly and unconsciously, and without knowledge of the underlying laws of Mental Influence, and those projected with a full knowledge of the laws governing the phenomena and urged on and directed by a powerful Will of the sender. The force is the same, but the degree of its power, and the measure of its effects are determined by the conditions of its sending force.

The vibratory force of these Thought-Waves does not cease with the sending forth of the wave, but persists for a long time afterward. Just as heat in a room persists long after the fire in the stove has been extinguished — just as the perfume of the flower exists in a room long after the flower has been removed — just as a ray of light travels through space for millions of miles, and for centuries after the star itself has been blotted out of existence — just as any and all forms of vibratory energy persist in manifesting after the initial impulse has been withdrawn — so do the vibrations of Thought continue long after the thought, yes, long after the brain which sent them forth has passed into dust.

There are many places today filled with the thought-vibrations of minds long since passed outside of the body. There are many places filled with the strong vibrations of tragedies long since enacted there. Every place has an atmosphere of its own, arising from the thought vibrations set in motion by the various persons who have inhabited or occupied them. Every city has its own mental atmosphere, which has an effect upon persons moving into them. Some are lively, some dull, some progressive, some old-fogeyish, some moral, some immoral — the result of the character of the early settlers and leading spirits of the places. The atmosphere affects persons moving into these towns, and either sinks to the general level, or else, if strong enough, help to change the mental tone of the place. Sometimes a change in conditions brings a large influx of new people to the town, and the mental waves of the newcomers tend to bring about a marked change in the local mental atmosphere. These facts have been noted by many observing people who were, perhaps, not familiar with the laws and principles underlying the phenomena.

Many have of course noticed the differing atmosphere of stores, offices and other places of business. Some of such places give one an air of confidence and trust; others create a feeling of suspicion and mistrust; some convey an impression of active, wide awake management, while others impress one as being behind the times and suffering from lack of alert, active management. Did you ever stop to think that these different atmospheres were caused by the prevailing mental attitudes of those in charge of the places? The managers of business places send forth Thought-Waves of their own, and their employees naturally falling into the pace set for them, sending forth similar vibrations, and before long the whole place is vibrating on a certain scale. Let a change in the management occur and see what a change soon manifests itself.

Did you ever notice the mental atmospheres of the houses you happened to visit? You may experience and recognize all of the varying notes in the mental scale of their occupants. From some thresholds harmony manifests itself, while others breathe in harmony as soon as you step over the threshold. Some radiate mental warmth, while others seem as cold as an iceberg. Think for a moment and recall the various houses or places you visit, and see how the mental vibrations of the inmates manifest themselves to a visitor.

The low quarters of our cities, the dens of vice and haunts of dissipation vibrate with the character of thought and feeling of those inhabiting them. And the weak-willed visitor is thus tempted. And, in the same way, certain places are filled with strong, helpful, elevating vibrations, which tend to lift up and elevate those coming within their circle of influence. Thoughts and Feelings are contagious, by reason of the Law of Vibration and Mental Induction. When this law is understood the individual is enabled to protect and improve himself. Such Knowledge brings Strength.

# Mental Induction

As we stated in the preceding chapter, the phenomena of Mental Influence bears a striking analogy to that of the electrical or magnetic energy. Not only is this so in the phase of wave motion and transmission, but also in the phase of induction, as we shall see presently.

In physical science the term Induction is used to indicate that quality in a manifestation of energy which tends to reproduce in a second object the vibrations manifesting in the first object, without direct contact between the two bodies. A magnet will induce magnetism in another object removed from its space. An electrified object will tend to produce similar vibrations in another object by induction, over great spaces. Heat waves travel along the ether, and tend to produce heat vibrations in objects far removed, notably in the case of the sun and the earth. Even sound waves will affect other objects in this way, as in the well-known instance of the glass or vase "singing" in response to the musical note sounded afar off. In fact, we see and hear by processes similar to those described.

And in this same manner that Thought-Waves carry the vibrations of the mind sending them forth to great distances, or lesser ones, tending to set up similar vibrations in the middle of other persons within their field force. Thus a person feeling a strong degree of anger will pour forth waves of that degree of mental vibration, which, coming in contact with the brains of other persons, tend to set up a similar feelings or emotions and thus cause the person to "feel cross" or "peevish" or even to manifest a similar angry state of mind. We all know how easily a fight is started by a very angry person in a room sending forth violent vibrations. One has but to remember the instances of mob violence to see how easily the "contagion of hate and anger" spread among people who allow themselves to be influenced. And not only is this true of undesirable emotions and feelings, but also of desirable ones. The influence of a good man who happens to be strong mentally spreads among those around him, influencing in them for good.

Orators, actors, preachers and teachers send forth strong within toll currents, which tend to produce mental conditions on the part of their hearers corresponding to the feeling held by the mind of the speaker. When you remember how this speaker swayed your feelings, or how that actor made you weep with pity, shiver with fear, or laugh with joy, you will see how Mental induction acts.

But not only is this true when we are in the actual presence of the person sending out the Thought-Waves, but it is equally true that we are influenced by persons far removed from us in space, often without their knowledge or intent, although sometimes (in the case of one who understands the principal most) with full knowledge and intent.

The ether with which space is filled carries these Thought-Waves in all directions, and the surface of the earth, particularly in the densely occupied portions, is filled with these waves. These waves, carrying the mental vibrations, coming in contact with each other, tend to set up combinations on one hand, or else neutralize each other on the other hand. That is to say, if two sets of waves of a similar nature meet there is likely to be a combination formed between them just as between two chemicals having an affinity for each other. In this way the "mental atmosphere" of places, towns, houses, etc., is formed. On the other hand if currents of opposing vibrations came in contact with each other, there will be manifested a conflict between the two, in which each will lose in proportion to its weakness, and the result will be either a neutralization of both or else a combination having vibrations of an average rate. For instance, if two currents of mental energy meet, one being a thought of Love and the other Hate, they will neutralize each other if they are equal, or if one is stronger than the other, it will persist but robbed of much of its strength. If it were not for this neutralizing effect we would be largely at the mercy of stray currents of thought. Nature protects us in this way, and also by rendering us immune to a considerable extent.

But nevertheless we are affected by these waves to a considerable extent, unless we have learned to throw them off by knowledge of the laws and an enforcement of them by practice. We all know how great waves of feeling spread over the town, city or country, sweeping people off their balance. Great waves of political enthusiasm, or War spirits, or prejudice for or against certain people, or groups of people, sweep over places and cause men to act in a manner that they will afterward regret when they come to themselves and consider their acts in cold blood. Demagogues will sway them or magnetic leaders who wish to gain their votes or
patronage; and they will be led into acts of mob violence, or similar atrocities, by yielding to these waves of "contagious" thought. On the other hand we all know how great waves of religious feeling sweep over a community upon the occasion of some great "revival" excitement or fervor.

The effect of these Thought-Waves, so far as the power of induction is concerned, of course depends very materially upon the strength of the thought or feeling being manifested in the mind sending them forth. The majority of persons put but little force into the mental manifestations, but here and there is to be found a thinker whose Thought-Waves are practically "a stream of living will" and which of course have a very strong inductive effect upon the minds of others with whom the waves come in contact. But it likewise follows that a number of persons thinking along the same lines will produce a great volume of power by a combination of their thought currents into great streams of mental force.

Then again there is another feature of the case that we must not lose sight of, and that is the Attraction between minds, by virtue of which one draws to himself the Thought-Waves of others whose thoughts are in accord with his own. The contrary is true, for there is Repulsion between the minds of persons and the Thought-Waves of others whose thoughts are not in accord with his own. The contrary is true, for there is Repulsions between the minds of persons and the Thought-Waves of others antagonistic to their thoughts. To quote a well-worn and much-used expression to illustrate this truth, "Like attracts Like," and "Birds of a Feather flock together." There is ever in operation this marvelous law of Attraction and Repulsion of Mental Energy— Persons allowing their thoughts to run along certain lines, and permitting the feelings to be expressed in certain ways, draw to themselves the Thought-Waves and mental influences of others keyed to the same mental key-note. And likewise they repel the waves and influences of an opposing nature. This is an important fact to remember in one's everyday life. Good attracts Good and repels Evil. Evil attracts Evil and repels Good. The predominant Mental Attitude serves to attract similar influences and to repel the opposing ones. Therefore watch carefully the character and nature of your thoughts — cultivate the desirable ones and repress the undesirable ones. Verily "As a man thinketh in his heart, so is he."

Some Thought-Waves sent forth with but little strength travel slowly and do not proceed very far from their place of emanation, but creep along like some smoke or fog, lazily and yielding. Other thoughts charged with a greater intensity of desire or will, dart forth vigorously like an electric spark, and often travel great distances. The weak Thought-Waves do not last a very long time, but fade away or become neutralized or dissipated by stronger, forces. But the strong thoughts persist for a long time, retaining much of their vitality and energy.

In the same manner the Thought-Waves of a person will continue to vibrate around him wherever he goes, and those coming in contact with him will be impressed by the character of his vibrations in this way. Some men send forth gloomy vibrations in this way. Some men send forth gloomy vibrations, which you feel when you come in contact with them. Others radiate good-cheer, courage and happiness, which conditions are induced in those with whom they come in contact. Many people will manifest these qualities so strongly that one can notice the effect the moment such persons enter a room. They carry their atmosphere with them, and the same is induced in the minds of others around them.

In the same way some people carry with them vibrations of Will-Power and Masterfulness that beat upon the minds of others, making them feel the power of such persons and conquering their own will-power and changing their desires. Others manifest a strong power of Fascination or Attraction, in a similar manner which tends to draw others to them and to their desires and wishes. Not only does this principle operate in the phase of general mental atmospheres, but also in the phase of direct personal influence.

All forms of Mental influence operate along the lines of Mental induction, as herein described. The principle is the same in all cases and instances, although the manner of operation varies according to the particular phase of the phenomena manifested. Remember this as we proceed, and you will be able to understand the subject much better.

# MENTAL CONCENTRATION

The two principal factors in the manifestation of Mental Influence, in all of its forms, are what are know as (1) Concentration, and (2) Mental Imagining. The first of these factors shall be considered in this chapter, the succeeding chapter taking up the consideration of the second.

"Concentration" is a word derived from two Latin words, i.e., "con," a prefix meaning " to;" and "centrum," meaning "center" or "fixed central point." The two words combined mean, literally, "to bring to a common point; to focus," etc. Thus the word "Concentration" is seen to mean, literally, "the act or state of bringing to a fixed point or focus.

Borrowing an analogous illustration from physical science, we readily see that the highest forms of energy, force or power are manifested by bringing the force to a focus, center, or common point thereby directing to that point the entire energy employed, instead of allowing it to become dissipated over a larger area. The electricity generated by a battery or dynamo, if allowed to diffuse itself over a large surface manifests but a small degree of the power that may be obtained from it by compelling it to discharge itself from a small point of focus. The same is true regarding the power of steam, which manifests great power by being forced to discharge itself
through a small point or opening instead of being permitted to spread itself widely in the air. The same law applies to gunpowder, which manifests force by its gases being compelled to escape through the small gun-barrel instead of spreading in all directions, which it would do if unconfined. Another familiar example is that of the sun glass, or "burning-glass," which brings the rays of the sun to a common point or focus, greatly intensifying the heat and light by reason thereof.

The occult masters have ever impressed upon their pupils the importance and necessity of acquiring the power of Mental Concentration, and all trained and developed occultists have practiced and persevered toward this end, the result being that some of them attained almost miraculous mental powers and influence. All occult phenomena are caused in this way, and all occult power depends upon it. Therefore the student of Mental Influence should devote much thought, time and practice to this most important branch of the subject.

It is a fact known to all students of mental phenomena that very few persons possess more than a very small degree of concentration. They allow their mental forces to become scattered and dissipated in all directions, and obtain little or no results from the same. In the degree that a man is able to concentrate, so is he able to manifests mental power. A man's power of mental concentration is to a great extent his measure of greatness.

Mental Concentration, in practice, consists of focusing the mind upon a given subject, or object, firmly and fixedly, and then holding it there for a certain time, fully intent upon its object, and not allowing itself to be diverted or attracted from its object. It likewise consists in the correlative power of then detaching the mind from that subject, or object, and either allowing it to rest, or else focusing it upon another object. In other words, it either gives undivided attention or else inhibits (or "shuts off") attention from the given subject or object.

To the reader who has had no experience along the lines of Mental Concentration, it may seem like a very easy Mental Influence task to focus the mind upon a subject, and then hold it there firmly and fixedly. But a little practice will undeceive such a person and will bring him to a realizing sense of the difficulty of the task. The mind is a very restless thing, and its tendency is to dance from one thing to another, darting here and there, soon tiring of continued attention, and like a spoiled child, seeking a new object upon which to exercise itself .On the other hand, many people allow their minds to concentrate (involuntarily) upon whatever may strike their fancy, and, forgetting everything else, they give themselves up to the object attracting their attention for the moment, often neglecting duties and important interests, and becoming day dreamers instead of firm thinkers. This involuntary concentration is a thing to be avoided, for it is the allowing of the attention to escape the control of the will. The Mental Concentration of the occultists is a very different thing, and is solely in control of the will, being applied when desirable, and taken off or inhibited when undesirable.

The trained occultist will concentrate upon a subject or object with a wonderful intensity, seemingly completely absorbed in the subject or object before him, and oblivious to all else in the world. And yet, the task accomplished or the given time expired, he will detach his mind from the object and will be perfectly fresh, watchful and wide-awake to the next matter before him. There is a difference in being controlled by involuntary attention, which is a species of self- hypnotizing, and the control of the attention, which is an evidence of mastery.

The secret of Mental Concentration lies in the control of the Attention. And the control of the Attention lies in the exercise of the Will.

A celebrated French psychologist has well said: "The authority is subject to the superior authority of the Ego. l yield it or I withhold it as

I please. l direct it in turn to several points. l concentrate it upon each point as long as my will can stand the effort." Sully says: "Attention may be roughly defined as the active self-direction of the mind to any object which presents itself at the moment."

All of the occult authorities begin teaching their pupils Attention as the first step toward Mental Concentration. They instruct the pupil to examine some familiar object, and endeavor to see as many details as possible in the object. Then after hearing the pupil's report, the master sends him back to the task, bidding him seek for new details, and so on until at last the pupil has discovered about all concerning the object that can be discovered. The next day a new object is given to him, and the process is repeated. First simple objects are given, and then more complex ones, until at last objects of great complexity are easily mastered. In this way not only is the power of close observation highly developed, but also the faculty of Attention becomes so highly strengthened that the pupil is able to exert the greatest amount of Mental Concentration with scarcely the consciousness of effort. And such a person then becomes a very giant in the manifestation of Mental Influence. For he is able to mold his mind "one-pointed," as the Orientals describe it, until he has focused and directed a mighty degree of Mental Influence toward the desired object.

Among the practices imposed upon their pupils by occult masters may be named Mathematics, Drawing, Analysis, etc. You will readily see why this is. To begin with, Mathematics requires the undivided attention of the student — unless he concentrates upon his examples, he will not be able to work out their solution. And, according to the principle in Nature that "practice makes perfect," and that "exercise develops power," the practice of the mind along lines requiring voluntary attention and mental concentration will inevitably result in the acquirement of the mental control and power, which renders possible the strongest manifestation of Mental Influence.

The person who uses Mental Influence must certainly possess the power of focusing the force to a common point, in order to manifest the greatest amount of power and influence. And that faculty of focusing results from the training of the mind along the lines of Concentration. And Concentration arises from the mastery of Voluntary Attention. So there you have the whole matter in a nutshell. So your first step toward acquiring Mental Influence should be to cultivate Voluntary Attention.

We might fill page after page with exercises designed to strengthen your faculty of Voluntary Attention, but what would be the use? The best plan is to set you to work to find something upon which to concentrate, for the very search will develop attention. Look around you for some object to study in detail. Then concentrate your attention upon it until you have seen all there is about it to be seen, then take up another object and pursue the practice further. Take a page — this page, if you will, and count the number of words on it. Then see how many words are required to fill each line, on an average, then see how many letters there are in each word, in each line, on the whole page. Then go over the page and see if any words are misspelled, or if any of the letters are imperfect, etc. In short, get acquainted with this page, until you know all about it. Then take up another page, and after studying it in the same way, compare the two. And so on. Of course this will be very dry and tedious unless you take an interest in it. And, remembering just what the exercise is designed for may arouse this interest. After practicing this way for a short time each day, you will begin to find that you are able to bestow greater

attention upon objects upon which you are trying to manifest Mental Influence. You are developing Concentration, and that is the great secret of the use of Mental Influence, and explains the difference in its manifestation among men. Think over this.

# MENTAL IMAGING

In our last chapter we called your attention to the first of the two principal factors in the manifestation of Mental Influence, namely, "Mental Concentration." In the present chapter we shall consider the second factor tending to render possible the said manifestation, namely, "Mental Imaging."

What is known as a "Mental Image, in occultism, is the mental creation, in the imagination of a "picture" of the things, events or conditions that one desires to be manifested or, materialized in actual effect. A moments thought will show you that unless you know "just what" you desire, you can take no steps toward attaining it on any plane of manifestation. And the more clearly your desires are perceived in your imagination, the clearer is the work of proceeding toward the realization of that desire. A Mental Image gives you a framework upon which to work. It is like the drawing of the architect, or the map of the explorer. Think over this for a few moments until you get the idea firmly fixed in your mind.

And now the same rule holds well on the plane in which the manifestation of Mental influence takes place. The occultist first builds up, in his imagination, a Mental Image or Picture of the conditions he wishes to bring about, and then by concentrating his influence strongly, instead of in a haphazard way as is the case with the majority of people who do not understand the laws and principles underlying the manifestations of the forces of mind. The Mental Image gives shape and direction to the forces, which is being concentrated upon the desired object or subject. It may be compared to the image on the glass of the Magic Lantern, through which the focused rays of the lamp pass, the result being that a corresponding image is reproduced upon the screen or curtain beyond. The analogy is a very close one indeed, if we remember that the minds of the majority of people are more or less blank screens or curtains upon which play the pictures produced there by outside influences, suggestions, environments, etc., for very few people realize their individuality, and are merely reflections of the thoughts and ideas of other people.

An eminent authority, Sir Francis Galton, who was one of the leading authorities upon psychology of preceding generations, has said on this subject: "The free action of a high visualizing faculty is of much importance in connection with the higher processes of generalized thought. A visual image is the most perfect form of mental representation whatever the shape, position and relations of objects to space are concerned. The best workmen are those who visualize the whole of what they propose to do before they take a tool in their hands. Strategists, artists of all denominations, physicists who contrive new experiments, and in short, all who do not follow routine, have a need for it. A faculty that is of importance in all technical and artistic occupations, that gives accuracy to our perceptions and justice to our generalizations, is starved by lazy disuse instead of being cultivated judiciously in such a way as will, on the whole, bring the best return. I believe that a serious study of the best way of developing and utilizing this faculty, without prejudice to the practice of abstract thought in symbols, is one of the many pressing desires in the yet unformed science of education."

And what Galton has said of the value of the use of this faculty of the mind in the affairs of the material plane, so it is likewise true of the manifestations on the mental plane. You know that the clearer a Mental Picture you possess of anything that you want — the better you know just what you want — and the better you know the latter, the better able you are to take steps to get it. Many people go through life wanting "something," but not really knowing "just what" they do want. Is it any wonder that they do not realize or materialize their desires any better? And the same thing holds well on the plane of manifestation of Mental Influence. If one wishes to materialize anything by the use of the influence, is he not handicapped by a lack of Mental Image of just what he wants to materialize, and is he not helped very much by the creation of a mental "pattern" or plan, in the shape of a mental picture, through and around which he may direct his thought-currents?

The occultists manifesting the greatest degree of Mental Influence acquire by practice this art of creating Mental Images of that which they wish to materialize. They train their Imagination in this way until the very act of creating the Mental Image acts strongly toward the actual materialization or event, as "actually existing" in their minds before they attempt to concentrate their Thought-Waves upon the task of accomplishing it. Then the Mental Picture, being completed and standing in strong outline, they focus their mental force through it, just as in the case of the magic lantern before referred to, and the picture is reproduced on the screen of mentality of other people.

The imagination may be strengthened in many ways, the principle being constant and persistent practice. The practice of recalling to the memory of scenes previously witnessed, and then whether describing them to others or else drawing a rough picture of them will help in this matter. Describe to others scenes that you have witnessed, occurrences. details of appearances, etc. etc., until you are able to reproduce mentally the aspects and appearances of the things. Then you may begin to draw mental pictures of things desired as if they were being drawn on the screen of your mind. See, mentally, the things as actually occurring — create a little playhouse of your own, in your mind, and there enact the plays that you wish to witness in actual life. When you have acquired this, you will be able to project your mental pictures on the screen of objectivity in actual life with far greater effect.

In thinking of this subject, you would do well to remember the illustration of the magic lantern, for the figure is a good one, and will enable you to carry the idea better in your mind. You see, in giving you this suggestion, we are really telling you to form a mental picture of the mental magic lantern, using the illustration given — you see how much easier it is for you to think of it in this way and how much easier it is for you to manifest it in practice.

Build your Mental Images by degrees, commencing with the general outlines, and then filling in the details. Always commence by trying simple and easy things, and then working up to the more complex and difficult feats.

And now, I offer a word of warning at this point to all. Do not allow your imagination to "run away with you" — do not became a dreamer of dreams and a doer of nothing. You must master your imagination and make it your servant and not your master. You must make it do your bidding, instead of allowing it to dictate to you.

You will see in the succeeding chapters the important part that Mental Imaging plays in the different phases of Mental Influence. Even when we do not refer directly to it by name, you will see that the "idea" sought to be conveyed by one mind to another — the feeling, desire or mental state sought to be transferred from one mind to others — must and does depend very materially for strength upon the dearness and completeness of the Mental Image held in the mind of the person seeking to do the influencing, the "projector" of the Mental Image of his mental magic lantern, upon the screen of the minds of others. Carry this principle well in mind that you may see its operation in the different forms.

# Fascination

In this and the next chapter we shall present to you information regarding the effect of Mental Influence manifested when there is personal contact between the persons using the power and the person affected. Then we shall pass on to a consideration of the effect produced when the persons are not in direct contact with each other.

There are two general forms of the direct use of Mental Influence, which, although somewhat resembling each other, may still be separated into two classes. The first we shall call "Fascination" and the second "Hypnotism."

By Fascination we mean the manifestation of Mental Influence when the two persons are together, without passes or the usual hypnotic methods. By Hypnotism we mean the use of the power, also, when the two parties are together, but accompanied by passes or hypnotic methods.

Under the head of Fascination are to be found the manifestations generally known as "Personal Magnetism," "Charming," etc., is quite commonly employed, in varying degrees by many persons, often without their conscious knowledge of the principles employed. Many persons are possessed of the power of Fascination "naturally" and without having studied or practiced the principles. Many others, not originally possessing the power, have acquired by study and practice the power to influence people in this way. For, it must be known, the power may be acquired by study and practice just as may any other power of mind and body. To some it is easy, to others difficult — but all may acquire a very great degree of the power by intelligent study and practice of the underlying principles.

Fascination is one of the oldest forms of the manifestations of Mental Influence. It was known to, and employed by, the earliest races of men. It is even found among the lower animals that pursue their prey or capture their mates by its use. A recent writer on the subject has defined the word, used in this connection, as: "Acting upon by some powerful or irresistible influence; influencing by an irresistible charm; alluring, exciting, irresistibly or powerfully, charming, captivating or attracting powerfully, influencing the imagination, reason or will of another in an uncontrollable manner; enchanting, captivating or alluring, powerfully or irresistibly."

As we have just said, this power is observable even among the lower animals in some cases. Instances are related by naturalists, which scorpions have fascinated other insects, causing them to circle around and around until finally the insect would plunge down right within striking distance of the scorpion, which would then devour its prey. Birds of prey unquestionably fascinate their game, and men who have been brought in contact with wild tigers, lions, etc., have testified that they felt paralyzed in some manner, their legs refusing to obey their will, and their minds seeming to become numbed and stunned. Those who have seen a mouse in the presence of a cat will testify to the effect of some power exerted by the latter. Birds in the presence of a cat and serpents also manifest symptoms of a conquered will. And naturalists cite many instances of the employment of this force by birds seeking to captivate and charm their mates at the beginning of the season.

Among men it has been noticed that certain individuals possess this power to a great degree. Some of the "great men" of ancient and modern times having been so filled with the power that they could manage their followers almost as one would move automatons. Julius Caesar had this power developed to a great degree, and used it from youth to his last days. He was worshipped — almost as a god by his soldiers — who would undertake almost any task at his bidding. Napoleon also possessed this charm to a wonderful degree. It enabled him to control men with whom he came in contact, and to bend them to his will. He rose from a poor student to the dignity and power of the Emperor of France. When banished to Elba he escaped, and landing in France, alone and unarmed, confronted the ranks of the French army drawn up to capture him, and walking towards the soldiers compelled the latter to throw down their guns and flock to his support. He entered Paris at the head of the great army, which had been sent forth to capture him. This is no wild legend, but a sober fact of history. And in our own times we see how certain leaders of men sweep people before them and move them around like pawns on the chessboard of life.

All of the above mentioned phenomena comes under the head of Fascination, and is the result of the emanation of streams of active Thought-Waves from the mind of a person, the same being strongly concentrated and directed toward those whom the person wishes to affect. The person forms a strong thought in his mind and sends it out to the others charged with the force of concentrated will, so that the other person feels it most strongly and forcibly. The fundamental idea is the forming of the thought, and then sending it out to the other person.

For instance, if you wish a person to like you, you should form in your mind this thought: "That person likes me," fixing it in your own mind as a fact. Then project to him the concentrated thought, "You like me — you like me very much," with an air of assurance and confidence, and the other person is bound to feel the effect unless he or she has acquired a knowledge of the subject and is using self-protection. The thought should be sent forth with the strength that usually accompanies a strong spoken statement, but you must not actually "speak" the words aloud — you should merely say them strongly "in your mind."

If you wish to produce an effect or impress Strength upon another person, the same process may be used, changing the Thought and vibrations to the idea that you have a stronger Will than the other person, and are able to overcome his Will — using the silent message of "I am Stronger than you — my Will overcomes yours,"

Some successful agents and salesmen use the following method in reaching their customers. They form a thought that the other person desires their goods very much, and then they send out the Thought-Waves that "You desire my goods — you want them very much — you have an irresistible longing for them," etc.

Others use the following when they wish another to comply with their wishes: "You will do as I say — will do as I say — you will yield to me fully and completely," etc.

You will readily see from the above examples that the whole principle employed in any and all of these cases consists of:

(1) The Thought of what the person wishes the other to do held firmly in the mind; and

(2) The projection of that Thought to the other, silently, in the shape of unspoken words.

In the above you have the whole secret of Fascination condensed to a small space. You will understand of course, that the words are only a means of concentrating and vitalizing the thought. Animals merely feel Desires, but are able to fascinate by the strength of them, although they cannot use words. And one person may fascinate another without understanding a word of his language, the real strength coming from the strength of the desire behind the words. The formation of the desire-thought into words, is merely for the purpose of concentrating and focusing the thought, for words are concentrated symbols of ideas, thoughts or feelings.

The exact process of "sending forth" the Thought-Wave to the other is difficult to describe. You know how you feel when you say something very forcible and emphatic to another person. You can fairly "feel" the force of the words being hurled at the other person. Well, cultivate that same power in sending forth the "unspoken word" in the above manner, and you will soon be able to notice the effect of the thought on the other.

It may help you to imagine that you can see the force flying from you to the other. The imagination properly used helps very much in these matters, for it creates a mental path over which the force may travel.

You must not act awkwardly when sending out the Thought-Waves, but converse in an ordinary manner, sending your Thought-Waves between your speeches, when the other person is talking to you, or at any pause in the conversation. It is always well to send first a powerful Thought-Wave before the conversation is opened, preferably while you are approaching the person. And it is likewise well to terminate the interview with a "parting shot" of considerable strength. You will find that these Thought-Waves are of far greater power than spoken words, and then again, you can in this way send out impressions that you could not utter in spoken words for obvious reasons.

And now do you see how you have been affected by persons who have influenced you at times in your past life? Now that you know the secret you will be in a measure immune from further impressions from others. And when you read our concluding chapter, entitled "Self-Protection," you will be able to surround yourself with a protective armor through which the Thought-Waves cannot penetrate, but which will turn aside the shafts directed toward you.

# Hypnotic Influence

As we have mentioned in the previous lesson, there is a general resemblance between the manifestation of Mental Influence, known as "Fascination," and that known as Hypnotic Influence. In the manifestation known as Fascination, the influence is exerted solely by Thought- Waves passing from mind to mind without a physical medium or channel other than the ether. In Hypnotic Influence, on the contrary, the influence is heightened by means of passes, stroking or eye influence.

In Hypnotic Influence the mind of the person affected, whom we shall call the "subject," is rendered passive by a flow of mental energy calculated to render it more or less drowsy or sleepy, and therefore less calculated to set up powers of resistance to the Thought-Waves of the person using the influence. But the power employed is the same in all cases, no matter whether they fall under the classification of Fascination or whether that of Hypnotic Influence. The two classes of manifestation, as a matter of fact, really blend into each other, and it is difficult to draw a dividing line in some cases.

Hypnotic Influence is a form of that which was formerly termed Mesmerism, which name was given to it in honor of its discoverer, Frederick Anton Mesmer, who practiced this form of Mental Influence during the latter half of the Eighteenth Century. As a fact, however, the force and its use was known to the ancients centuries before Mesmer's time, the latter person having merely rediscovered it.

Mesmer taught that the power was based upon the presence of a strange universal fluid which pervaded everything, and which had a peculiar effect upon the nerves and brains of people. He and his followers believed that it was necessary to put the subjects into a sound sleep before they could be influenced. But both of these ideas have given way to the new theories on the subject now held by investigators and students of the subject.

It is now known that the "magnetic fluid" believed in by Mesmer and his followers is nothing else than the currents of Thought-Waves emanating from the mind of the operator. And it is also known that the "deep sleep" condition is not necessary to render the will of the subject subservient to that of the operator. It is also now known that the nerves of the arms and fingers afford a highly sensitive conductor for the mental currents, which may be propelled over them to the mind of the subject, or to his nerves and muscles. This fact is explained by the well-known scientific fact that the material of which the nerves are composed is almost identical with that of the brain — in fact the nervous system may be spoken of as a continuation of the brain itself. It is now also known that the eye has a peculiar property of transmitting the mental currents along the rays of light entering it and from thence to the eyes of the other person. The above fact explains the phenomena of hypnotic influence, as it is now known to science. The question of "Suggestion" also has a bearing on the subject, as we shall see presently.

Modern operators do not produce the "deep sleep" condition usually except in cases when it is desired to produce some form of psychic phenomena apart from the subject of Mental Influence — that is, in which they are merely inducing the deep hypnotic condition in order to get the subject into a psychic condition in which the phenomena mentioned may be manifested or exhibited. We shall not enter into this phase of the subject in this book, for it is outside of the immediate subject. The modem hypnotic investigator merely induces a passive state in the mind, nerves or muscles of the subject sufficient to reduce the powers of resistance, and then he gives his orders or "verbal suggestions" accompanied by a projection of his Thought-Waves into the mind of the subject.

In order to illustrate the subject, we will give you a few experiments, which may be easily performed by anyone manifesting the power of concentration and thought-projection. There is of course a great difference in the degrees of impressionability of different persons to hypnotic influence — that is to say, difference in degrees of resistance. Some persons will interpose a strong resistance, while others will set up a very feeble resistance, which is easily beaten down by the will of the operator. In the following experiments you had better begin by getting some person who is perfectly willing for the experiment, and who will not interpose a resistance but who is willing to become passive. Some person friendly to you and interested in the experiments, we mean.

Begin by having the person stand before you. Then make sweeping passes in front of the person from head to foot. Then make a few passes in front of the face of the subject, then along his arms. Then take hold of his hands and hold them a little while, looking him straight in the eyes. Make all passes downward. Avoid levity or laughter and maintain a serious, earnest expression and frame of mind.

Then standing in front of the subject tell him to take his will off of his legs and stand perfectly passive and relaxed. Then looking him straight in the eyes, say to him: "Now, I am going to draw you forward toward me by my mental power — you will feel yourself falling forward toward me — don't resist but let yourself come toward me — I will catch you, don't be afraid - now come - come - come - now you're coming, that's right," etc. You will find that he will begin to sway toward you and in a moment or two will fall forward in your arms. It is unnecessary to say that you should concentrate your mind steadily upon the idea of his falling forward, using your will firmly to that effect. It will help matters if you hold your hands on each side of his head, but just in front of him, not touching him, however, and then draw away your hands, toward yourself, saying at the same time: "Come now come — you're coming," etc. Standing behind the subject and drawing him backward may reverse this experiment. Be sure and catch him in your arms when he fails to protect him from a fall to the floor.

In the same manner you may fasten his hands together, telling him that he cannot draw them apart. Or you may start him revolving his hands, and then giving him orders that he cannot stop them. Or you may draw him all around the room after you, following your finger that you have pointed at his nose. Or you may make him experience a feeling of heat and pain by touching your finger to his hand and telling him that it is hot. All of the familiar simple experiments may be performed successfully upon a large percentage of persons, in this way, by following the above general directions. We shall not go into detail of the higher experiments of Hypnotism, as that forms a special subject by itself. We give the above experiments merely for the purpose of showing you that the phenomena of Hypnotic Influence does not require any "magnetic fluid" theory, and is all explainable upon the hypothesis of Mental Influence by means of Thought- Waves and Mental Induction.

In the above experiments, be sure you "take off" the influence afterward, by making upward passes, and willing that the influence pass off. Do not neglect this.

In your experiments, if you care to undertake them, you will soon discover the power of your eye upon the other persons. You will be able to almost feel the force passing from your gaze to theirs. And this is true in the case of the passes and stroking of the hands. You will feel the vibratory waves flowing from your hands into their nervous system. It is wonderful what power is aroused in a person after conducting a few experiments along these lines. Those who care to follow the subject further are referred to a forthcoming book of this series, to be issued shortly, and which will be called "The New Hypnotism," in which full instructions will be given in the higher phenomena, in complete detail.

And now a word of warning — Beware of people who are always putting their hands on you, or patting or stroking you, or wishing to hold your hands a long time. Many persons do this from force of habit, and innocently, but others do so with the intention of producing a mild form of hypnotic influence upon you. If you meet such persons, and find them attempting anything of this sort, you can counteract their influence by sending them a strong thought current (as stated in our last chapter), sending them the thought: "You can't affect me — I am too strong for you — you can't play your tricks on me." It is a good plan to practice this counteracting force when you are shaking hands with a "magnetic" person who seems to affect people. You will soon be able to distinguish these people by a certain force about them and a peculiar expression in their eyes, at the same time using your protective will upon them.

Caution young girls against allowing young men to be too free in using their hands in caressing them, and a word of advice to young men in your family would not be out of place in this respect. There are many cases of sex-attraction, leading to very deplorable results, arising from a conscious or unconscious use of this simple form of Hypnotic Influence. The danger lies in the fact that it renders one passive to other influences, and more readily led into temptation and to yield to the desires or will of the other person. A word to the wise should be sufficient. The use of this power for immoral purposes is a terrible crime and brings down upon the user deplorable results, which all occultists know and teach. Everyone should learn to resist such influences when exerted upon them. Forewarned is Forearmed.

# INFLUENCING AT A DISTANCE

In the two preceding chapters we invited your consideration of the manifestation of Mental Influence when the user or projector of the force was in actual contact with, or in presence of, the person or persons he was aiming to influence. In this chapter, and the one immediately following it, we shall pass on to a consideration of the manifestation of the influence when the persons affected are removed in space from the person using the influence.

The general public is familiar in a general way with the phenomena of hypnotism. and to a lesser degree with the phenomena of Fascination in its more common forms of personal Magnetism, etc. But as regards the use of the influence at a distance people are more or less skeptical owing to a lack of knowledge of the subject. And still every day is bringing to the mind of the public new facts and instances of such an influence. and the teaching of various cults along these lines is now awakening a new interest in the subject, and a desire to learn something regarding the laws and principles underlying the same.

As strange as it may appear at first glance, the principles underlying Mental Influence at a distance are precisely the same as those underlying the use of influence when the persons are in the presence of each other. A little thought must show the truth of this. In the case of present influence the mental-currents flow across an intervening space between the two minds — there is a space outside of the two minds to be traversed by the currents. And a moment's thought will show you that the difference between present influence and distant influence is merely a matter of degree — a question of a little more or less space to be traversed by the currents. Do you see this plainly?

Well, then, this being so, it follows that the methods used must be identical. Of course, in the case of personal influence the added effect of the voice, manner, suggestive methods, the eye, etc., are present, which render the result more easily obtained, and causes the "rapport" condition to be more easily established. But with this exception the methods are identical, and even the advantages accruing from the exception mentioned may be duplicated by practice and development in the case of distant influence.

There are a number of methods given by the authorities in this matter of distant influencing, but they are all based upon the same principles named in the previous chapters of this book, i.e. Vibrations,

Thought-Waves, Mental Induction, Concentration and Mental Imaging — in these words you have the key to the subject — the rest is all a matter of practice and development, and variation.

One of the most elementary, and yet one of the most effective methods known to occultists is that of creating a Mental Image of the person "treated" (for that is the common term among modern writers on the subject) in the sense of imagining him to be seated in a chair in front of the person treating him at a distance. The treater proceeds to give both verbal commands, and at the same time directs Thought-Waves toward the imaginary person seated before him. This process establishes a psychic condition between the treator and the actual person, although the latter may be removed from the treator by many miles of space. This was the method of the ancient magicians and wonder-workers, and has always been a favorite among persons pursuing these experiments, of desirous, of mentally influencing others at a distance.

A variation of the above, very common in former days, was to mold a clay or wax figure, calling it by the name of the person treated, and identifying it in the mind and imagination with the other person. A variation is also noticed in the cases where a photograph, lock of hair, article of clothing, etc., is used in this way as a psychic connecting link between the two persons. The practitioners of Black Magic, Witchcraft and of her nefarious perversions of Mental influence seemed to prefer these methods, although, on the contrary, they are used with the very best results today by many in giving beneficial treatments to absent patients, friends and others whose welfare is desired. The only effect the Mental Image of the person, or the picture, etc., has is the fact that by these means a psychic connection link is set up along which the Thought- Waves travel more readily.

In the above forms of treatment the treator treats the Mental Image, picture, etc., precisely as he would if the person were actually present. He forgets for the time being that the person may be hundreds of miles away, and concentrates his influence on the image, or picture, etc., because the latter is really the starting point of the psychic chain, which leads direct to the person. The treator sends his Thought-Waves toward the object, and in some cases actually talks (mentally) to the person by means of the medium mentioned. He may give commands, arguments, remonstrance, persuasion, etc., just as if the person were actually present. In short, he acts as if the person were sitting before him, wide-awake, and receptive to his influence.

Another way, employed by some, is to begin darting Thought-Waves toward the other person, forming in the imagination a gradual lengthening "psychic-wire" composed of thought- vibrations. Those practicing this form state that when the psychic-wire is projected sufficiently far (and it travels with incredible speed) and comes in contact with the mind of the other person, the treator feels at once that contact has been established by a peculiar faint "shock" similar to that of a very mild galvanic current. Then the treator proceeds to send his thought-currents along the psychic-wire in the same manner as if the person were actually in his presence, as described under the head of "Fascination, in a preceding chapter. In fact, such treatments, and the others mentioned in this chapter, are really and practically "long distance Fascination."

Another form of distant treatment consists in forming an "astral-tube," mentioned in other books in this series. The astral-tube is set up in a similar manner to the "psychic-wire," and projected toward the person desired to influence. It is formed in the imagination as a "vortex-ring," similar to the little ring of smoke puffed out by the cigar smoker, only larger — about six inches to one foot wide — or, better still, like the ring of smoke ejected from the stack of a locomotive sometimes when it is puffing rapidly. This vortex-ring is then seen, in the imagination, by the use of the will, to lengthen out in the shape of a tube which rapidly extends and travels toward the person treated, in a manner identical with that of the psychic-wire. This tube is known to occultists as the "astral-tube," and is employed in various forms of occult and psychic phenomena, such as clairvoyance and other forms of "Psychomancy," as described by us in our volume of this series, so entitled. Those following this method of distant influencing report that they recognize the completion of the tube by a sensation of stoppage and a feeling of "rapport" having been established between themselves and the other person. In some cases they report that they are able to faintly "see" the figure of the other person in miniature at the other end of the tube, but this is undoubtedly due to the possession of "psycho-mantic" powers, suddenly awakened in to effect. The tube once established the treatment is proceeded with as if they were in the actual presence of the person treated. In many respects the "psychic-wire" and the "astral-tube" methods are similar, and a statement concerning one is generally true of the other.

There are two other methods frequently used in distant influencing which we shall now briefly describe.

The first of these two methods consists in sitting or standing in a quiet place, or rather in some place in which you can concentrate (the advanced occultist can find peace in the midst of the noise) and then directing your Thought-Waves toward the other person, forming in the imagination a mental picture of the force flying from you toward the other, like tiny sparks of electricity, or of a subtle fluid. This mental picture tends to give a concentrative force to the current, which renders them powerful, and sends them direct to the desired spot.

The second of these two methods is that used by the most advanced occultists who have advanced beyond the use of the methods described just now. These people simply stand or sit quietly and concentrate their minds until they attain the state of Mental Calm known to many as "the Silence." Then they create a strong mental picture of the person treated, surrounded by the conditions desired created, or doing the things desired to be done. This is one of the highest forms of Mental Influence and really approaches a higher phase of influence than that of the mental plane as generally known. A picture of a person held in the mind in this way — the person being seen in perfect, robust health, and happy and successful — tends to materialize the same conditions in the person in real life. This form of treatment, however, is possible only to those of great concentration, and who have mastered the act of Mental Imaging, and who also possess Creative Will-Power to a marked degree. Some degree of success in it, however, is open to nearly every student who practices along these lines.

Before practicing any of these experiments, read what we have said in the chapter on "Magic Black and White, and guard against employing the power for evil purposes, for the fate of the Black Magician is a sad one.

# INFLUENCING "EN MASSE"

In our last chapter we considered the manifestation of Mental Influence at a distance in so far as was concerned the influencing of one or more persons by another. There is another phase of the subject that must not be overlooked, and that is the influencing of large numbers of people by some active, strong projector of Mental Influence. This form of the manifestation of the power is known as "Mental Influencing En Masse" — "En Masse, of course, means "in a body" — or "in a crowd," and Mental Influencing En Masse means the use of the influence in the phase of exerting a strong attracting or directing power to the mind of "the crowd," or rather, "the public, or a large number of people.

This form of the use of the power is that consciously or unconsciously exerted by the great leaders of men in the fields of statesmanship, politics, business, finance or military life. You will at once recall a number of the so called "great men" of history from ancient times down to our own times who seemed to exert a wonderfully, almost miraculous, effect upon the minds of the people, causing men to see things through the eyes of the strong man, and making of all instruments to carry out the ideals, will or desires of these great masters of Mental Influence. And on a smaller scale are the majority of the successful people who depend upon public support. In fact, this influence in some degree is used by nearly all who succeed in any form of business or profession, in which success calls for the attraction of other people toward the occupation of the person in question. This may seem like a strange thought to many, but occultists know it as the truth, notwithstanding.

The most common form of Influencing En Masse is the lesser degree manifestation, along unconscious lines, manifested by a majority of people by reason of their desire for the success of certain things. By desire we do not mean the mere "wanting" or "wishing" state of mind, but rather that eager longing, craving, demanding mental state that evinces a hungry reaching out for the desired thing. You will notice that the men and women who "get things" are generally those who are possessed of a strong, burning desire for the things in question, which prompts them to be more of less aggressive in the search for satisfaction of the desire possessing them. These people are constantly sending out strong waves of thought-vibrations, which has a drawing, attracting influence upon all with whom they come in contact, and tending to draw such persons toward the center of attraction, which is, of course, the mind of the person sending out such thoughts. And in the same way a person possessed of a strong Fear of a thing will send out similar attracting waves, which have a tendency to attract or draw to him the people calculated to bring about the materialization of the thing feared. This may sound paradoxical, but the secret lies in the fact that in both the case of Desire and Fear the mind forms the Mental Image, which tends to become materialized. Fear, after all, is a form of "expectation," which, alas, too, often tends to materialize it." The thing that I have feared, hath come upon me," says Job, and in that saying he has stated the experience of the race. The way to fight things you may fear is to create a burning desire for the opposite thing.

Other persons who have either studied the principles of Mental Influence, or else have stumbled upon certain facts concerning the same, improve upon this elementary form of Influencing En Masse just mentioned. They send out the Thought-Waves consciously and deliberately, erecting the mental image, and holding strongly to it, so that in time their sweeps of mental currents reach further and further away and bring a greater number of people under the influence and into the field of attraction. They "treat" the public "en masse" by holding the strong mental picture of that which they desire, and then sending out strong thought-currents of desire in all directions, willing that those coming within their radius shall be attracted toward the ideas expressed in the Mental image projected in all directions.

The constant dwelling upon some special object or subject, by men who have developed concentration, strong wills and fixity of purpose, has the effect of sending out from the mind of that person great circles, constantly widening, of Thought-Waves, which sweep ever outward like waves in a pond caused by dropping in a stone. These waves reach and affect a great number of people, and will render them at least "interested" in the object or subject thought of, and the indifference has been overcome. Other appeals to the minds of these people will be far more likely to reach them than otherwise, for "interest" is the first step toward attention, and attention is another step toward action.

Of course, there are very many people sending out circles of Thought-Waves, and these currents come in contact with each other and tend to neutralize each. But now and then a particularly strong man will send out waves that will persist even after meeting other currents, and will reach the minds of the public in spite of the opposition. These thought-currents have the personality of the sender, and reflect the character of his will, be it strong or weak. The Mental Influence sent out by a strong business man in a town will soon make itself felt in a subtle manner, and the store becomes a center of attractive influence, although the public does no understand just why. In the same way some lawyers spring into public favor, although not possessing greater ability than their legal brethren. And popular preachers make their influence felt in a community in similar ways, although often they are not conscious of just what force they are using, their only knowledge being that they have a feeling of inward strength and an attractive influence over people, and at the same time a burning ardent desire to draw people their way, and a strong will to back it up with. And these are just the mental qualities that create and manifest the strongest kind of Mental Influence. And besides, these people almost invariably "know just what they want" — there is no mere vague "wishing" about them — they make a clear mental picture of the things that they wish to bring about, and then they bend every effort toward materializing the picture. Everything they do towards accomplishing their ends gives an additional impetus to their constantly widening and constantly strengthening circle of power and influence.

Some masters of this art of influencing the public create a mental picture of themselves sending out great volumes of Thought-Waves for a time, and then afterward mentally imparting a rotary motion to the waves, until at last they form a mental whirlpool rushing round and round and always sucking in toward the center. An effort of this kind acts on the mental plane just as a physical whirlpool acts on the physical plane, that is it draws into its power all that comes in contact with its force. This is one of the most powerful forms of Influencing En Masse, and is used with great effect by many of the "strong men" of this age; who have acquainted themselves fully with the secrets of the ancient occultists. Ancient Occultism and Modern Finance seem far apart, but they are really working together to further the interests of some of these powerful minds of the day — and the public is paying the bill.

You will readily see from what has been said that an individual who has cultivated the faculty of concentration and has acquired the art of creating sharp, clear, strong mental images, and who when engaged in an undertaking will so charge his mind with the idea of success, will be bound to become an attracting center. And if such an individual will keep his mental picture ever in his mind, even though it may be in the background of his mind, when he is attending to the details and planning of his affairs — if he will give his mental picture a prominent place in his mental gallery, taking a frequent glance at it, and using his will upon it to create new scenes of actual success, he will create for himself a center of radiating thought that will surely be felt by those coming within its field of influence.

Such a man frequently "sees" people coming to him and his enterprises and falling in line with his plans. He mentally "sees" money flowing in to him, and all of his plans working out right. In short, he mentally imagines each step of his plans a little ahead of the time for their execution and he concentrates forcibly and earnestly upon them. It is astonishing to witness how events, people, circumstances and things seem to move in place in actual life as if urged by some mighty power to serve to materialize the conditions so imaged in the mind of the man. But, understood, there has got to be active mental effort behind the imaging. Daydreamers do not materialize thought — they merely dissipate energy. The man who converts thought in activity and material being, throws energy into the task and puts forth his willpower through the picture on the slide. Without the rays of the will there will be no picture projected, no matter how beautifully the imagination has pictured it. Thoughts pictured in mental images and then vitalized by the force of the desire and will tend to objectify themselves into material beings, That is the whole thing in a nutshell.

# THE NEED OF THE KNOWLEDGE

Although the true scientific principles underlying the subject of Mental Influence have been but recently recognized and taught to the general public, still the knowledge is far from being new. The occultists of the old civilizations undoubtedly understood the underlying principles and used them in practice, thus gaining an ascendancy over the masses. And more than this, the masses themselves had a more or less comprehensive knowledge of the working principles of the subject, for we find among all peoples, in all times, records of the use of this power. Under one name or another — under one form or another — Mental Influence has been operated and used from the earliest times. And today, even in the most remote portions of the globe, and among the most savage and barbarous races we find instances of the employment of this force.

The forms of the manifestation of Mental Influence are many and varied. In some cases it manifests under the form of a fascinating, attracting power exerted by some people, which causes such persons to draw or attract other persons to them. Persons are allured or "charmed" by others possessing this power, and their affections are taken captive by this mysterious force. Some persons are spoken of as "fascinating," "possessing powers of charming," having "winning ways," having "great personal magnetism," etc. Others exert another form of the power in the driving of and compelling others to do their bidding, and people speak of them as having "a
compelling will," being able "to work their will" on those around them, possessing "dominating powers," etc. We are also brought face to face with the wonderful effects of "Mental Science" under one form or another, under this name or that term, with the many forms of "treatments" followed by the different schools and cults. Then we read in the pages of history about the mysterious powers recorded under the name of Witchcraft, Hexes, Voodoo's, and Black Magic, including the Hawaiian "Kahuna" work. And turning back the pages of history to Ancient time, Greece, Persia and Egypt, not to speak of India, ancient and modern, we find innumerable instances of the employment of, and knowledge of, Mental influence in some of its forms.

And although many will seek to deny the fact, scientific investigators and students realize that there is but one real underlying principle under and back of all of the various forms of manifestation. The good results, and the evil results, all arise from the employment of the same force, strange as it may appear at first thought. The secret lies in the fact that this Mental Influence is a great natural force, just as is electricity or any other natural forces, and it may be, and is, used for both good and evil purposes. The electricity which runs out machines, lights our houses and performs countless other beneficent tasks in the service of man is also used to electrocute criminals, and the unfortunate person who touches a "live wire" may be struck with instant death. The sun, which warms our earth and renders life possible, also kills countless persons exposed to its rays on the desert, or even in our large cities. Fire, that great friend of man, which has been one of the most potent factors in the evolution of the race from barbarism to civilization, is also a mighty enemy, destroying both property and lives. Water, that most necessary element, which renders life possible, and which is necessary to grow our grain and to perform countless other good services for us, also acts as an enemy at times, drowning people and sweeping away their homes. Gravitation, which holds all things in place, from suns and stars down to the tiniest atom of matter, also causes people to fall to their death from high places, or brings down on their heads objects from above them. In short, every natural force or power is capable of producing either beneficent or baleful effects to man, according to the circumstances of the case. We recognize these things, and accept them as a law of nature. And yet some would deny the identity of the power of Mental influence as manifested in its good and bad uses.

There will be people who ascribe to God all the good qualities of Mental Influence, and ascribe to the Devil all of its evil uses. These people have primitive minds. Their counterparts are seen in those who would credit God with the helpful rain or sun, and who ascribe to the Devil the same things when there occurs a flood or a drought. Such reasoning is worthy only of the savage mind. The forces are natural forces, and work according to their own laws, imminent in their constituent qualities and nature, and are in that sense "above good and evil." When they work for man's interest and comfort man calls them "good" — when they work harm and discomfort to him man call them "bad" — but the force remains unchanged, being neither "good" nor "bad." And thus it is with the power of Mental Influence — it is above "good" and "bad" — it is a great natural force, capable of being used for either wear or woe to mankind. But, remember this, there is a difference. While the force in itself is neither good nor bad the individual who employs it may be, and it is, "good" or "bad," according to its use. Just as a man commits a good or bad act when he uses his gun to slay a wild beast attacking another man, or else turns it upon his brother or neighbor, as the case may be — so is a man good or bad according to his use of Mental Influence. The merit or demerit lies in the intention and purpose of the user, not in the force or power employed by him. Therein lies the difference.

On all sides of us we may see the manifestation of the possession of Mental Influence. We see men who are able to sway those around them in some mysterious and wonderful way, either by their powers of persuasion of by their dominant will power. Some spring into prominence and power suddenly, in a way unaccountable to those who are ignorant of the secret of Mental Influence. As we have said in a previous chapter, certain people seem to have "something about them" that makes them attractive or successful in their relations with other people. The "personal magnetism" of leaders manifests itself strongly, some having this power to such an extent that the masses follow them like a great flock of sheep after the "bell-whether" with the tinkling bell around his neck.

We have all come in contact with the "agent" or salesman who managed in some way to sell us things that we did not want and had no use for, and after he had gone we wondered and wondered how it all happened. If we had but understood the laws of Mental Influence this could not have happened. We have all felt ourselves, at some time or another in our lives, in the presence of individuals who almost compelled us to do what we knew in our hearts we should not do. Knowledge of the laws of Mental influence would have enabled us to overcome the temptation.

And not only in the case of personal interviews have we been affected. There is a far more subtle and dangerous use of the power, i.e., in the shape of "distant influence," or "absent treatment," as it had been called. And the increase in the interest and knowledge of Occult matters during the past twenty years has resulted in a widely diffused knowledge of this great force, and its consequent employment, worthily and unworthily, by many people who are thereby enabled to gain an influence over their neighbors and fellow men, who are not familiar with the laws of the force. It would surprise many people if they knew that some of the multi-millionaires of the country, and some of its greatest politicians and leaders, were secret students of Occultism, and who were using their forces upon the masses of the people.

Not only this, but there are Schools of Occultism which teach their pupils the theory, practice and art of Mental Influence, under one name or another — under this guise or that — the result being that there are a greater number of people equipped for the use of this force and instructed in the practice of employing it turned out every year than is generally imagined. There are Schools for Salesmanship giving disguised instruction in the art of Mental Influence. Nearly every large concern employing selling agents has private instructors for their men, who teach them the principles of Mental Influence disguised under the name of "Psychology of Business," or some such name.

And besides these, there are a number of people who have studied at the feet of some of the great metaphysical, semi-religious cults of the day, who have received instruction in Mental influence disguised under the name of some creed or religious teachings, who have departed from the moral principles inculcated by their by their teachers, and who are using their knowledge in the shape of "treatments" of other persons for the purpose of influencing them to accede to their wishes or to act so as to bring financial gain to the person giving the treatment. The air is full of this Black Magic today, and it is surely time that the general masses were instructed on this subject. And this is the purpose of this little book, published and sold at a popular price in order to bring it within the reach of the purses of the "plain people," who have been exploited and influenced by those who have acquired a knowledge of the principles of Mental Influence, and who are using it unworthily upon their fellow men.

There is self protection possible to all, and this little book purposes to teach you how to use it.

# MAGIC BLACK AND WHITE

The use of the word "Magic" in connection with Mental Influence is quite ancient. Occultists make a clear distinction between the use of Mental Influence in a manner conducive to the welfare of others, and its use in a selfish, base manner calculated to work harm on others. Both forms are common and are frequently mentioned in all occult writings.

White Magic has many forms, both in its ancient manifestations and in these latter days of revived occult knowledge. The use of Mental Influence in this way generally takes the form of kindly "treatments" of persons by others having their welfare at heart. In this particular class fall the various treatments of the several cults and schools of what is known as Mental Science, or similar names. These people make a practice of giving treatments, both "present" and "absent," for the purpose of healing physical ailments and bringing about a normal Physical condition of health and strength. Similar treatments are given by some to bring about a condition of Success to others, by imparting to the minds of such persons the vibrations of courage, confidence, energy, etc., which surely make for success along the lines of material occupation, etc.

in the same way one may "treat" adverse conditions surrounding others, bringing the force of the mind and will to bear on these conditions with the idea of changing the prevailing vibrations and bringing harmony from in-harmony, and success from failure.

The majority of persons, not informed along these lines, are surrounded by a mental atmosphere arising from the prevailing mental states, thoughts, feelings, etc., and also arising from the thought-currents which have attracted to them by the Law of Mental Attraction. These Mental Atmospheres, when once firmly settled around a person, render it most difficult for him to "break away" from their vibrations. He struggles and fights, but the prevailing vibrations are beating down upon him all the time and must produce a strong effect upon even persons of strong will, unless indeed they have fully acquainted themselves with the laws of Mental influence and have acquired the power of Concentration. The habit of a lifetime, perhaps, has to be overcome, and besides the constant suggestive vibrations from the mental atmosphere are constantly bringing a pressure to bear upon the person, so that indeed he has a mighty task before him to throw off the old conditions, unaided and alone. And, so, while individual effort is preferable, there comes a time in the lives of many people when "a helping hand," or rather a "helping mind," is of great service and aid.

The person coming to the mental aid of a person needing his or her services is performing a most worthy and proper act. We hear a great deal about "interfering with other people's minds" in such kind and worthy "treatments," but in many cases there is but little real interference done. The work of the helper is really in the nature of neutralizing and dissipating the unfavorable. Mental Influence surrounds the other person, and thereby giving the other person a chance to work out his own mental salvation. It is true that everyone must do his or her own work, but help of the kind above indicated is surely most worthy and proper.

In these White Magic treatments the person giving the treatments forms the Mental Picture of the desired condition in his mind, and then sends his thought-currents to the other person endeavoring to reproduce the Mental Picture in the mind or thought-atmosphere of the other person. The best way of doing this, of course, is to assert mentally that the desired condition actually exists. One may be of great help and aid to others in this way, and there is no good reason why it should not be done.

And now for the reverse side of the shield — We wish it were possible to avoid even a mention of this hateful form and manifestation of Mental Influence, but we feel that ignorance is no protection, and that it is useless and foolish to pursue the policy of the ostrich which sticks its head in the sand when pursued, that not seeing the hunter the latter may not see him. We believe that it is better to look things in the face, particularly where it is a case of "forewarned being forearmed."

It is a fact known to all students of occultism that Black Magic has been frequently employed in all times to further the selfish, base aims of some people. And it is also known to advanced thinkers today that even in this enlightened age there are many who do not scruple to stoop to the use of this hateful practice in order to serve their own ends, notwithstanding the punishment that occultists know awaits such persons.

The annals of history are full of records of various forms of witchcraft, conjuration and similar forms of Black Magic. All the much talked of forms of "putting spells" upon people are really forms of Black Magic, heightened by the fear and superstition of those affected.

One has but to read the history of witchcraft to see that there was undoubtedly some force at work behind all of the appalling superstition and ignorance shown by the people of those times. What they attributed to the influence of people "in league with the devil" really arose from the use of Black Magic, or an unworthy use of Mental Influence, the two things being one. An examination of the methods used by these "witches," as shown by their confessions, gives us a key to the mystery. These "witches" would fix their minds upon other people, or their animals, and by holding a concentrated mental picture there, would send forth Thought-Waves affecting the welfare of the persons being "adversely treated," which would influence and disturb them, and often bring on sicknesses. Of course, the effect of these "treatments" were greatly heightened by the extreme ignorant fear and superstition held by the masses of people at the time, for Fear is ever a weakening factor in Mental influence, and the superstitions and credulity of the people caused their minds to vibrate in such a manner as to render them extremely passive to the adverse influences being directed against them.

It is well known that the Voodoos of Africa, and similar cults among other savage races, practice Black Magic among their people with great effect. Among the natives of Hawaii there are certain men known as "Kahunas," who pray people sick, or well, whichever way they are paid for. These instances could be multiplied had we the space and inclination to proceed further with the matter.

And in our own civilized lands there are many people who have learned the principles of Mental Influence, and who are using the same for unworthy purposes, seeking to injure others and defeat their undertakings, or else trying to bring them around to their own (the "treator's") point of view and inclinations. The modern revival of occult knowledge has operated along two lines. On the one hand we see and hear of the mighty power for good Mental Influence is exerting among the people today, raising up the sick, strengthening the weak, putting courage into the despondent and making successes of failures. But on the other hand the hateful selfishness and greed of unprincipled persons in taking advantage of this mighty force of nature and prostituting it to their own hateful ends, without heeding the dictates of conscience or the teaching of religion or morality. These people are sowing a baleful wind that will result in their reaping a frightful whirlwind on the mental plane. They are bringing down upon themselves pain and misery in the future.

At this point we wish to utter a solemn warning to those who have been, or are tempted, to employ this mighty force for unworthy purposes .The laws of the mental plane are such that "as one sows so shall he reap." The mighty Law of Attraction acts with the accuracy of a machine, and those who seek to entangle others in a net of Mental influence sooner or later are caught by their own snare. The Black

Magician involves him to pieces. He is sucked down into the whirlpool of his own making, and is dragged down to the lowest depths. These are not idle remarks, but a statement of certain laws of nature, in operation on the mental plane, which all should know and heed.

And to those who may feel appalled at this mention of the existence and possibilities of Black Magic we would say that there is one thing to be remembered, and that is that GOOD always overcomes EVIL on the mental plane. A good thought always has the power to neutralize the Evil one, and a person whose mind is filled with Love and Faith may combat a multitude whose minds are filled with Hate and Evil. The tendency of all nature is upward and toward Good. And he who would pull it back toward Evil sets himself against the law of Spiritual Evolution, and sooner or later falls a victim to his folly.

And then, remember this: Thought-Waves find entrance only to those minds that are accustomed to think similar thoughts. He who thinks Hate may be affected by Hate thoughts, while he whose mind is filled with Faith and Love is surrounded by a resistant armor which repels the invading waves, and causes them to be deflected, or else driven back to their senders. Bad thoughts, like chickens, come home to roost. Thoughts ace like Boomerangs, in their tendency to return to their sender. To the poison of Black Magic Nature gives the antidote of Right-Thinking.

# Self-Protection

The reader of the preceding chapters will see the power of Mental Influence in its various phases of manifestation, and will recognize the possibility of the force being used to influence himself. The question that will naturally arise in the mind of every student and investigator of this important subject, and which comes to all at sometime, is: "How may I protect myself from the use of this power against myself — how may I render myself immune from these influences which may be directed against me?"

It is true that we, and other writers on the subject, have shown you that one is far less liable to influence if he will maintain a mental atmosphere of high vibration — that is keeping oneself surrounded by a thought atmosphere filled with vibrations of the highest kind of thoughts and free from thoughts and desire of a base, selfish character, which tends to attract similar thoughts. In this way one creates a state of mental hygienic cleanliness which renders him immune from the "contagious thoughts of the selfish plane of desire," etc. This should be remembered and taken advantage of by everyone, for just as physical cleanliness gives no congenial lodgment for the germs of disease, so mental cleanliness refuses to admit the mental microbes.

But there is a method far more efficacious than even the above-mentioned plan. And this method is really that employed by the adepts in Occultism, and the method and practice taught the initiates of the occult brotherhoods and lodges all over the world. Let us consider it here.

In the first place, without entering into a statement of the details of the high occult teachings, we wish to inform you that the Basic Principle of all such teaching and instruction is the fact that within each of us, in the very center of the being of each individual — in the very heart of hearts of the immortal Ego — is what occultists know as the Flame of the Spirit. This is what you recognize in consciousness as the "I *am*" consciousness — that consciousness of being which is far above the consciousness of Personality, or the things of personality. It is that consciousness which informs each individual, unmistakably, that he IS actually an Individual Being. This consciousness comes to the individual by reason of his contact with the great One Life of the Universe — it is the point of contact between the *part* and the *all*.

And in this part of a man's consciousness, coupled with the sense of *being* and "I," there resides a spark from the Divine Flame of Life and Power, which is what has been called the *will* of man. Now, do not mistake us and confuse this with the so called Will of personality, which is merely a Desire, or else a certain firmness, which often is little more than Stubbornness. This inner Will is Real Power, and when once recognized may be drawn upon as a source of unending and unfailing Strength. The occult adepts have developed the consciousness of this Power Within, and use it freely. This is the result of years of practice, and correct living and thinking. But, still, each and every person may draw upon this source of strength within them to aid them in life and to repel the thought-vibrations of the lower plane.

This consciousness may be developed by a realization of its existence, and by a practice of bringing the idea in everyday consciousness, by thought, meditation and practice. The very fact of having called your attention to its existence has awakened within the mind of You who are reading these lines a new strength and sense of power. Think a moment and see whether you do not feel a dawning sense of Strength within you that you have not realized so fully before this moment! A continued recognition in your everyday consciousness of this Something Within will develop your ability to manifest it. Particularly in an hour of need will it spring to your assistance, giving you a sense of a part of yourself crying out to you in words of encouragement: "I Am Here! Be Not Afraid!"

It is very difficult to give you this method in written or printed works, but if you will enter fully into a recognition of this Inward Power you will find yourself developing a new power of resisting outside influences that will astonish you.

When you come in contact with people who are seeking to influence you in any of the ways mentioned in the preceding chapters of this book, or in others ways, you will find yourself able to defy their mental attacks by simply remembering the strength imminent in your "I," aided by the statement (made silently to yourself): "I am an Immortal Spirit, using the Will within my Ego." With this Mental Attitude you may make the slightest mental effort in the direction of throwing out from your mind vibrations, which will scatter the adverse influences in all directions, and which, if persisted in, will cause the other person to become confused and anxious to let you alone.

With this consciousness held in mind, your mental command to another, "Let me alone — I cast off your influence by the power of my Spirit," will act so strongly that you will be able to actually see the effect at once. If the other person is stubborn and determined to influence you by words of suggestion, coaxing, threatening, or similar methods, look him or her straight in the eyes, saying mentally "I defy you — my inner power casts off your influence. Try this the next time that anyone attempts to influence you either verbally or by Thought-Waves and see how strong and positive you will feel, and how the efforts of the other person will fail. This sounds simple, but the little secret is worth thousands of dollars to every individual who will put it into practice.

Above all, put out of your mind all Fear of others persons. The feeling of fear prevents you from manifesting the power within you to its full extent. Cast out fear as unworthy and hurtful.

Not only the case of personal influence in the actual presence of the other person may be defeated in this way, but the same method will act equally as well in the matter of repelling the mental influence of others directed against you in the form of "absent treatments," etc. If you feel yourself inclining toward doing something which in your heart you feel that is not to your best interests, judged from a true standpoint, you may know that, consciously or unconsciously someone is seeking to influence you in this way. Then smile to yourself and make the statements mentioned above, or some similar one, and holding the power of the Spirit within your "I" firmly in you mind, send out a mental command just as you would in the case of the actual presence of the person himself or herself. You may also deny the influencing power out of existence by asserting mentally: "I *deny* your power to influence me — you have no such power over me — I am resting on my knowledge of Spirit and its Will within me — I deny your power out of existence." This form of denial may be used either in the case of absent influence or personal influence. The rule is the same in all cases.

In repelling these absent influences you will at once experience a feeling of relief and strength and will be able to smile at the defeated efforts of the other person. If you feel sufficiently broad and full of love for mankind you may then "treat" the other person for his error, sending him thoughts of Love and Knowledge with the idea of dispelling his ignorance and selfishness, and bringing him to a realization of the higher truths of life.

You will doubtless have many interesting experiences arising from thus repelling these attacks. In some cases you will find that the next time you meet the person in question he will appear confused and puzzled and ill at ease. In other cases the person will begin to manifest a new respect and regard for you, and disposed to aid you instead of trying to influence you to his way and desire. In other cases the person will still have the desire, and will endeavor to "argue" you into doing that which he has tried to influence you into doing by Mental Influence, but his efforts will "fall flat," and without effect, particularly if you give him "another dose of the assertion of the Power of the Spirit within you.

In the same way you should call upon your Higher Self for aid and strength when you feel yourself being affected by any of the great Mental Waves of feeling or emotion sweeping over the public mind, and which have a tendency to "stampede" people into adopting certain ideas, or of following certain leaders. In such case the assertion of the "I" within you will dissipate the influence around you, and you will find yourself standing in a center of Peace surrounded on all sides by the ocean of mental tumult and agitation which is sweeping over or circling around the place. In the same way you will be able to neutralize the unpleasant mental atmospheres of places, localities, houses, etc., and render yourself positive to and immune from the same. n short, we have given you here a recipe that may be used in any and every instance of the employment of Mental Influence. It may sound simple to you, but a little use of it will make you deem it the most important bit of practical knowledge you may possess.

# The Power of Concentration

Written under the pen name Theron Q. Dumont

## Table of Contents

*exercise. The real benefit of physical culture usually lost sight of. How to hold the facilities at work.*

*within all of us. How to make plans work out. The mightiest power in the world is free for you to use. The motive power which supplies the energies necessary for achievement.*

*The man that can concentrate is well poised. What you must do to be successful today. Concentration that is dangerous. How to make those you come in contact with feel as you do. The man that becomes a power in the world. You can control your life and actions. Successful lives are the concentrated lives. Why people do not get what they "concentrate" on.*

*Habit is but a powerful enemy and wonderful ally of concentration. Most people are controlled through the power of habit. Most people are imitators and copiers of their past selves. All physical impressions are the carrying out of the actions of the will and intellect. How everyone could be made happier and successful. Some wonderful maxims. Habit the deepest law of human nature. How to overcome undesirable habits. Some special instructions by Dr. Oppenheim.*

*A successful business not the result of chance. Failure not caused by luck. The intense desire that is necessary to make a business a success. Those that achieve permanent success deserve it. The man that is able to skilfully manage his business. How to realize your ambition. The successful business attitude. Your opinion should be as good as any one else. How many ruin their judgment. The man that gets the best results. A successful business not hard to build up; may be built up In a few years now whereas formerly it took a lifetime. How to do more and better work. How to attract the ideas thought out by others. Many attract forces and Influences that they should not. Broaden the visions of those you come in contact with.*

*Lack of courage creates financial, as well as mental and moral difficulties. The man without courage attracts all that is contemptible, weakening, demoralizing and destructive. It is just as easy to be courageous as cowardly. Courage concentrates the mental forces on the task at hand. Cowardice dissipates both mental and moral forces. How to banish doubts. No one knows what they can do until they try. Once you understand the law everything is possible. How to build up courage to do as you wish. Difficulties soon melt away before the courageous.*

*foreign to most people. How to concentrate on what you want and get it. The miraculous help we apparently receive at times. How one man started a business on thirteen cents and in six years built up a business that pays him $6,000 a year. When you put forth the necessary concentrated effort you will receive great help from unknown sources.*

*Your happiness and success depends upon your ideals. A valuable lesson. Through concentration we can work out our ideals In physical life. What a different world this would be if we would build the right kind of ideals. Every time you change your ideal you think differently. Life is one continuous unfoldment. You can be happy every step of its way or miserable as you please. How our grandest thoughts come to us.*

*An inventor's vision. Why It is easy to project your thoughts to another. How your mental powers can draw to you forces of a helpful nature. The big business man must possess mental power of control. How to make a friend or relative succeed. How to generate enthusiasm and the spirit of success. Your environment is either helpful or harmful. Mental starvation. How to instil your thoughts and ideas into others. Influence that must be shaken off before you can advance. Our attitude has more to do with success than you realize.*

*A most effective and practical method of developing the Will. Practical exercises. Will training without exercises. Will-power can overcome big obstacles. The Will to win. Man an unknown quality until his powers are developed. Ability plentiful, but organizing, initiative and creative power not so plentiful. The driving force within.*

*Those unable to concentrate will generally suffer from poverty and unhappiness, The best instructor will only help you to the extent you put it into practice. Gaining the mastery of your work, life powers and forces. Concentrate the dominant quality that makes men successful. Everyone can learn to concentrate better. An experiment to try. Final instructions.*

# Introduction

We all know that in order to accomplish a certain thing we must concentrate. It is of the utmost value to learn how to concentrate. To make a success of anything you must be able to concentrate your entire thought upon the idea you are working out.

Do not become discouraged, if you are unable to hold your thought on the subject very long at first. There are very few that can. It seems a peculiar fact that it is easier to concentrate on something that is not good for us, than on something that is beneficial. This tendency is overcome when we learn to concentrate consciously.

If you will just practice a few concentration exercises each day you will find you will soon develop this wonderful power.

Success is assured when you are able to concentrate for you are then able to utilize for your good all constructive thoughts and shut out all the destructive ones. It is of the greatest value to be able to think only that which will be beneficial.

Did you ever stop to think what an important part your thoughts, concentrated thoughts, play in your life? This book shows their far-reaching and all-abiding effects.

These lessons you will find very practical. The exercises I have thoroughly tested. They are arranged so that you will notice an improvement from the very start, and this will give you encouragement. They point out ways in which you can help yourself.

Man is a wonderful creature, but he must be trained and developed to be useful. A great work can be accomplished by every man if he can be awakened to do his very best. But the greatest man would not accomplish much if he lacked concentration and effort. Dwarfs can often do the work of giants when they are transformed by the almost magic power of great mental concentration. But giants will only do the work of dwarfs when they lack this power.

We accomplish more by concentration than by fitness; the man that is apparently best suited for a place does not always fill it best. It is the man that concentrates on its every possibility that makes an art of both his work and his life.

All your real advancement must come from your individual effort.

This course of lessons will stimulate and inspire you to achieve success; it will bring you into perfect harmony with the laws of success. It will give you a firmer hold on your duties and responsibilities.

The methods of thought concentration given in this work if put into practice will open up interior avenues that will connect you with the everlasting laws of Being and their exhaustless foundation of unchangeable truth.

As most people are very different it is impossible to give instructions that will be of the same value to all. The author has endeavored in these lessons to awaken that within the soul which perhaps the book does not express. So study these lessons as a means of awakening and training that which is within yourself. Let all your acts and thoughts have the intensity and power of concentration.

To really get the full benefit of these lessons you should read a page, then close the book and thoughtfully recall its ideas. If you will do this you will soon cultivate a concentrated mental habit, which will enable you to read with ordinary rapidity and remember all that you read.

# Lesson I: Concentration Finds the Way

Everyone has two natures. One wants us to advance and the other wants to pull us back. The one that we cultivate and concentrate on decides what we are at the end. Both natures are trying to gain control. The will alone decides the issue. A man by one supreme effort of the will may change his whole career and almost accomplish miracles. You may be that man. You can be if you Will to be, for Will can find a way or make one.

I could easily fill a book, of cases where men plodding along in a matter-of-fact way, were all at once aroused and as if awakening from a slumber they developed the possibilities within them and from that time on were different persons. You alone can decide when the turning point will come. It is a matter of choice whether we allow our diviner self to control us or whether we will be controlled by the brute within us. No man has to do anything he does not want to do. He is therefore the director of his life if he wills to be. What we are to do, is the result of our training. We are like putty, and can be completely controlled by our will power.

Habit is a matter of acquirement. You hear people say: "He comes by this or that naturally, a chip off the old block," meaning that he is only doing what his parents did. This is quite often the case, but there is no reason for it, for a person can break a habit just the moment he masters the "I will." A man may have been a "good-for-nothing" all his life up to this very minute, but from this time on he begins to amount to something. Even old men have suddenly changed and accomplished wonders. "I lost my opportunity," says one. That may be true, but by sheer force of will, we can find a way to bring us another opportunity. There is no truth in the saying that opportunity knocks at our door but once in a lifetime. The fact is, opportunity never seeks us; we must seek it. What usually turns out to be one man's opportunity, was another man's loss. In this day one man's brain is matched against another's. It is often the quickness of brain action that determines the result. One man thinks "I will do it," but while he procrastinates the other goes ahead and does the work. They both have the same opportunity. The one will complain of his lost chance. But it should teach him a lesson, and it will, if he is seeking the path that leads to success.

Many persons read good books, but say they do not get much good out of them. They do not realize that all any book or any lesson course can do is to awaken them to their possibilities; to stimulate them to use their will power. You may teach a person from now until doom's day, but that person will only know what he learns himself. "You can lead him to the fountain, but you can't make him drink."

One of the most beneficial practices I know of is that of looking for the good in everyone and everything, for there is good in all things. We encourage a person by seeing his good qualities and we also help ourselves by looking for them. We gain their good wishes, a most valuable asset sometimes. We get back what we give out. The time comes when most all of us need encouragement; need buoying up. So form the habit of encouraging others, and you will find it a wonderful tonic for both those encouraged and yourself, for you will get back encouraging and uplifting thoughts.

Life furnishes us the opportunity to improve. But whether we do it or not depends upon how near we live up to what is expected of us. The first of each month, a person should sit down and examine the progress he has made. If he has not come up to "expectations" he should discover the reason, and by extra exertion measure up to what is demanded next time. Every time that we fall behind what we planned to do, we lose just so much for that time is gone forever. We may find a reason for doing it, but most excuses are poor substitutes for action. Most things are possible. Ours may be a hard task, but the harder the task, the greater the reward. It is the difficult things that really develop us, anything that requires only a small effort, utilizes very few of our faculties, and yields a scanty harvest of achievement. So do not shrink from a hard task, for to accomplish one of these will often bring us more good than a dozen lesser triumphs.

I know that every man that is willing to pay the price can be a success. The price is not in money, but in effort. The first essential quality for success is the desire to do--to be something. The next thing is to learn how to do it; the next to carry it into execution. The man that is the best able to accomplish anything is the one with a broad mind; the man that has acquired knowledge, that may, it is true, be foreign to this particular case, but is, nevertheless, of some value in all cases. So the man that wants to be successful must be liberal; he must acquire all the knowledge that he can; he must be well posted not only in one branch of his business but in every part of it. Such a man achieves success.

The secret of success is to try always to improve yourself no matter where you are or what your position. Learn all you can. Don't see how little you can do, but how much you can do. Such a man will always be in demand, for he establishes the reputation of being a hustler. There is always room for him because progressive firms never let a hustler leave their employment if they can help it.

The man that reaches the top is the gritty, plucky, hard worker and never the timid, uncertain, slow worker. An untried man is seldom put in a position of responsibility and power. The man selected is one that has done something, achieved results in some line, or taken the lead in his department. He is placed there because of his reputation of putting vigor and virility into his efforts, and because he has previously shown that he has pluck and determination.

The man that is chosen at the crucial time is not usually a genius; he does not possess any more talent than others, but he has learned that results can only be produced by untiring concentrated effort. That "miracles," in business do not just "happen." He knows that the only way they will happen is by sticking to a proposition and seeing it through. That is the only secret of why some succeed and others fail. The successful man gets used to seeing things accomplished and always feels sure of success. The man that is a failure gets used to seeing failure, expects it and attracts it to him.

It is my opinion that with the right kind of training every man could be a success. It is really a shame that so many men and women, rich in ability and talent, are allowed to go to waste, so to speak. Some day I hope to see a millionaire philanthropist start a school for the training of failures. I am sure he could not put his money to a better use. In a year's time the science of practical psychology could do wonders for him. He could have agencies on the lookout for men that had lost their grip on themselves; that had through indisposition weakened their will; that through some sorrow or misfortune had become discouraged. At first all they need is a little help to get them back on their feet, but usually they get a knock downwards instead. The result is that their latent powers never develop and both they and the world are the losers. I trust that in the near future, someone will heed the opportunity of using some of his millions in arousing men that have begun to falter. All they need to be shown is that there is within them an omnipotent source that is ready to aid them, providing they will make use of it. Their minds only have to be turned from despair to hope to make them regain their hold.

When a man loses his grip today, he must win his redemption by his own will. He will get little encouragement or advice of an inspiring nature. He must usually regain the right road alone. He must stop dissipating his energies and turn his attention to building a useful career. Today we must conquer our weakening tendencies alone. Don't expect anyone to help you. Just take one big brace, make firm resolutions, and resolve to conquer your weaknesses and vices. Really none can do this for you. They can encourage you; that is all.

I can think of nothing, but lack of health, that should interfere with one becoming successful. There is no other handicap that you should not be able to overcome. To overcome a handicap, all that it is necessary to do is to use more determination and grit and will.

The man with grit and will, may be poor today and wealthy in a few years; will power is a better asset than money; Will will carry you over chasms of failure, if you but give it the chance.

The men that have risen to the highest positions have usually had to gain their victories against big odds. Think of the hardships many of our inventors have gone through before they became a success. Usually they have been very much misunderstood by relatives and friends. Very often they did not have the bare necessities of life, yet, by sheer determination and resolute courage, they managed to exist somehow until they perfected their inventions, which afterwards greatly helped in bettering the condition of others.

Everyone really wants to do something, but there are few that will put forward the needed effort to make the necessary sacrifice to secure it. There is only one way to accomplish anything and that is to go ahead and do it. A man may accomplish almost anything today, if he just sets his heart on doing it and lets nothing interfere with his progress. Obstacles are quickly overcome by the man that sets out to accomplish his heart's desire. The "bigger" the man, the smaller the obstacle appears. The "smaller" the man the greater the obstacle appears. Always look at the advantage you gain by overcoming obstacles, and it will give you the needed courage for their conquest.

Do not expect that you will always have easy sailing. Parts of your journey are likely to be rough. Don't let the rough places put you out of commission. Keep on with the journey. Just the way you weather the storm shows what material you are made of. Never sit down and complain of the rough places, but think how nice the pleasant stretches were. View with delight the smooth plains that are in front of you.

Do not let a setback stop you. Think of it as a mere incident that has to be overcome before you can reach your goal.

# Lesson II: the Self-mastery: Self-direction Power of Concentration

Man from a psychological standpoint of development is not what he should be. He does not possess the self-mastery, the self-directing power of concentration that is his by right.

He has not trained himself in a way to promote his self-mastery. Every balanced mind possesses the faculties whose chief duties are to engineer, direct and concentrate the operations of the mind, both in a mental and physical sense. Man must learn to control not only his mind but his bodily movements.

When the controlling faculties (autonomic) are in an untrained condition, the impulses, passions, emotions, thoughts, actions and habits of the person suffer from lack of regulation, and the procedure of mental concentration is not good, not because the mind is necessarily weak in the autonomic department of the faculties, but because the mind is not properly trained.

When the self-regulating faculties are not developed the impulses, appetites, emotions and passions have full swing to do as they please and the mind becomes impulsive, restless, emotional and irregular in its action. This is what makes mental concentration poor.

When the self-guiding faculties are weak in development, the person always lacks the power of mental concentration. Therefore you cannot learn to concentrate until you develop those very powers that qualify you to be able to concentrate. So if you cannot concentrate one of the following is the cause:

1. "Deficiency of the motor centers." 2. "An impulsive and emotional mind." 3. "An untrained mind."

The last fault can soon be removed by systematic practice. It is easiest to correct.

The impulsive and emotional state of mind can best be corrected by restraining anger, passion and excitement, hatred, strong impulses, intense emotions, fretfulness, etc. It is impossible to concentrate when you are in any of these excited states.

These can be naturally decreased by avoiding such food and drinks as have nerve weakening or stimulating influences, or a tendency to stir up the passions, the impulses and the emotions; it is a very good practice to watch and associate with those persons that are steady, calm, controlled and conservative.

Correcting the deficiency of the motor centers is harder because as the person's brain is undeveloped he lacks will power.

To cure this takes some time. Persons so afflicted may benefit by reading and studying my course, "The Master Mind."[*]

[*] To be published by Advanced Thought Publishing Co., Chicago, Ill.

Many have the idea that when they get into a negative state they are concentrating, but this is not so. They may be meditating, though not concentrating. Those that are in a negative state a good deal of the time cannot, as a rule, concentrate very well; they develop instead abstraction of the mind, or absence of mind. Their power of concentration becomes weaker and they find it difficult to concentrate on anything. They very often injure the brain, if they keep up this state. To be able to concentrate you must possess strength of mind. The person that is feeble-minded cannot concentrate his mind, because of lack of will. The mind that cannot center itself on a special subject, or thought, is weak; also the mind that cannot draw itself from a subject or thought is weak. But the person that can center his mind on any problem, no matter what it is, and remove any unharmonious impressions has strength of mind. Concentration, first, last and all the time, means strength of mind.

Through concentration a person is able to collect and hold his mental and physical energies at work. A concentrated mind pays attention to thoughts, words, acts and plans. The person who allows his mind to roam at will will never accomplish a great deal in the world. He wastes his energies. If you work, think, talk and act aimlessly, and allow your brain to wander from your subject to foreign fields, you will not be able to concentrate. You concentrate at the moment when you say, "I want to, I can, I will."

Some Mistakes Some People Make. If you waste your time reading sensational stories or worthless newspaper items, you excite the impulsive and the emotional faculties, and this means you are weakening your power of concentration. You will not be a free engineer, able to pilot yourself to success.

Concentration of the mind can only be developed by watching yourself closely. All kinds of development commence with close attention. You should regulate your every thought and feeling. When you commence to watch yourself and your own acts and also the acts of other people, you use the faculties of autonomy, and, as you continue to do so, you improve your faculties, until in time you can engineer your every thought, wish and plan. To be able to focalize the mind on the object at hand in a conscious manner leads to concentration. Only the trained mind can focalize. To hold a thought before it until all the faculties shall have had time to consider that thought is concentration.

The person that cannot direct his thoughts, wishes, plans, resolutions and studies cannot possibly succeed to the fullest extent. The person that is impulsive one moment and calm the next has not the proper control over himself. He is not a master of his mind, nor of his thoughts, feelings and wishes. Such a person cannot be a success. When he becomes irritated, he irritates others and spoils all chances of any concerned doing their best. But the person that can direct his energies and hold them at work in a concentrated manner controls his every work and act, and thereby gains power to control others. He can make his every move serve a useful end and every thought a noble purpose.

In this day the man that gets excited and irritable should be looked upon as an undesirable person. The person of good breeding now speaks with slowness and deliberation. He is cultivating more and more of a reposeful attitude. He is consciously attentive and holds his mind to one thing at a time. He shuts out everything else. When you are talking to anyone give him your sole and undivided attention. Do not let your attention wander or be diverted. Give no heed to anything else, but make your will and intellect act in unison.

Start out in the morning and see how self-poised you can remain all day. At times take an inventory of your actions during the day and see if you have kept your determination. If not, see that you do tomorrow. The more self-poised you are the better will your concentration be. Never be in too much of a hurry; and, remember, the more you improve your concentration, the greater are your possibilities. Concentration means success, because you are better able to govern yourself and centralize your mind; you become more in earnest in what you do and this almost invariably improves your chances for success.

When you are talking to a person have your own plans in mind. Concentrate your strength upon the purpose you are talking about. Watch his every move, but keep your own plans before you. Unless you do, you will waste your energy and not accomplish as much as you should.

I want you to watch the next person you see that has the reputation of being a strong character, a man of force. Watch and see what a perfect control he has over his body. Then I want you to watch just an ordinary person. Notice how he moves his eyes, arms, fingers; notice the useless expenditure of energy. These movements all break down the vital cells and lessen the person's power in vital and nerve directions. It is just as important for you to conserve your nervous forces as it is the vital forces. As an example we see an engine going along the track very smoothly. Some one opens all the valves and the train stops. It is the same with you. If you want to use your full amount of steam, you must close your valves and direct your power of generating mental steam toward one end. Center your mind on one purpose, one plan, one transaction.

There is nothing that uses up nerve force so quickly as excitement. This is why an irritable person is never magnetic; he is never admired or loved; he does not develop those finer qualities that a real gentleman possesses. Anger, sarcasm and excitement weaken a person in this direction. The person that allows himself to get excited will become nervous in time, because he uses up his nerve forces and his vital energies. The person that cannot control himself and keep from becoming excited cannot concentrate.

When the mind can properly concentrate, all the energy of every microscopic cell is directed into one channel and then there is a powerful personal influence generated. Everyone possesses many millions of little trembling cells, and each one of these has a center where life and energy are stored up and generated. If this energy is not wasted but conserved and controlled, this person is influential, but when it is the opposite, he is not influential or successful.

Just as it is impossible for a steam engine to run with all its valves open, so is it impossible for you to waste your energy and run at your top speed. Each neuron in the gray layers of the brain is a psychic center of thought and action, each one is pulsating an intelligent force of some kind, and when this force, your thoughts and motions, are kept in cheek by a conservative, systematic and concentrated mind, the result will be magnetism, vitality and health. The muscles, bones, ligaments, feet, hands and nerves, etc., are agents for carrying out the mandates of the mind. The sole purpose of the volitional faculties is to move the physical mechanism as the energy travels along the wires of nerves and muscles. Just for that reason, if you throw a voluntary control over these messages, impulses, thoughts, emotions, physical movements and over these physical instruments you develop your faculties of self-mastery and to the extent you succeed here in proportion will you develop the power of concentration.

Any exercise or work that excites the mind, stimulates the senses, calls the emotions and appetites into action, confuses, terrifies or emotionalizes, weakens the power of concentration. This is why all kind of excitement is bad. This is the reason why persons who drink strong drinks, who allow themselves to get into fits of temper, who fight, who eat stimulating food, who sing and dance and thus develop their emotions, who are sudden, vehement and emotional, lack the power to concentrate. But those whose actions are slower and directed by their intelligence develop concentration. Sometimes dogmatic, wilful, excitable persons can concentrate, but it is spasmodic, erratic concentration instead of controlled and uniform concentration. Their energy works by spells; sometimes they have plenty, other times very little; it is easily excited; easily wasted. The best way to understand it is to compare it with the discharge of a gun. If the gun goes off when you want it to, it accomplishes the purpose, but if it goes off before you are ready for it, you will not only waste ammunition, but it is also likely to do some damage. That is just what most persons do. They allow their energy to explode, thus not only wasting it but endangering others. They waste their power, their magnetism and so injure their chance of success. Such persons are never well liked and never will be until they gain control over themselves.

It will be necessary for them to practice many different kinds of concentration exercises, and to keep them up for some time. They must completely overcome their sudden, erratic thoughts, and regulate their emotions and movements. They must from morning to night train the mind to be steady, and direct and keep the energies at work.

The lower area of the brain is the store house of the energy. Most all persons have all the dynamic energy they need if they would concentrate it. They have the machine, but they must also have the engineer, or they will not go very far. The engineer is the self-regulating, directing power. The person that does not develop his engineering qualities will not accomplish much in life. The good engineer controls his every act. All work assists in development. By what you do you either advance or degenerate. This is a good idea to keep always in mind. When you are uncertain whether you should do something or not, just think whether by doing it you will grow or deteriorate, and act accordingly.

I am a firm believer in "work when you work, and play when you play." When you give yourself up to pleasure you can develop concentration by thinking of nothing else but pleasure; when your mind dwells on love, think of nothing but this and you will find you can develop a more intense love than you ever had before. When you concentrate your mind on the "you" or real self, and its wonderful possibilities, you develop concentration and a higher opinion of yourself. By doing this systematically, you develop much power, because you cannot be systematic without concentrating on what you are doing. When you walk out into the country and inhale the fresh air, studying vegetation, trees, etc., you are concentrating. When you see that you are at your place of business at a certain time each morning you are developing steadiness of habit and becoming systematic. If you form the habit of being on time one morning, a little late the next, and still later the following one, you are not developing concentration, but whenever you fix your mind on a certain thought and hold your mind on it at successive intervals, you develop concentration.

If you hold your mind on some chosen object, you centralize your attention, just like the lens of the camera centralizes on a certain landscape. Therefore always hold your mind on what you are doing, no matter what it is. Keep a careful watch over yourself, for unless you do your improvement will be very slow.

Practice inhaling long, deep breaths, not simply for the improvement of health, although that is no small matter, but also for the purpose of developing more power, more love, more life. All work assists in development.

You may think it foolish to try to develop concentration by taking muscular exercises, but you must not forget that the mind is associated with muscle and nerve. When you steady your nerves and muscles, you steady your mind, but let your nerves get out of order and your mind will become erratic and you will not possess the power of direction, which, in other words, is concentration. Therefore you understand how important exercises that steady the nerves and muscles are in developing concentration.

Everyone is continually receiving impulses that must be directed and controlled if one is to lead a successful life. That is the reason why a person must control the movements of his eyes, feet, fingers, etc.; this is another reason why it is important to control his breathing. The slow, deep, prolonged exhalations are of wonderful value. They steady the circulation, the heart action, muscles and nerves of the mind. If the heart flutters, the circulation is not regular, and when the lung action is uneven, the mind becomes unsteady and not fit for concentration. This is why controlled breathing is very important as a foundation for physical health.

You must not only concentrate your mind, but also the action of the eyes, ears and fingers. Each of these contain miniature minds that are controlled by the master engineer. You will develop much quicker if you thoroughly realize this.

If you have ever associated with big men, or read their biographies, you will find that they usually let the others do the talking. It is much easier to talk than it is to listen. There is no better exercise for concentration than to pay close attention when some one is talking. Besides learning from what they have to say, you may develop both mental and physical concentration.

When you shake hands with some one just think of your hand as containing hundreds of individual minds, each having an intelligence of its own. When you put this feeling into your hand shake it shows personality. When you shake hands in a listless way, it denotes timidity, lack of force and power of personality. When the hand grip is very weak and stiff, the person has little love in his nature, no passion and no magnetism. When the hand shake is just the opposite, you will find that the nature is also. The loveless person is non-magnetic and he shows that he is by his non-magnetic hand shake. When two developed souls shake hands, their clasps are never light. There is a thrill that goes through both when the two currents meet. Love arouses the opposite currents of the positive and negative natures. When there is no love, life loses its charm. The hand quickly shows when love is being aroused. This is why you should study the art of hand shaking and develop your social affections. A person that loves his kind reflects love, but a person that hates reflects hate. The person with a bad nature, a hateful disposition, evil thoughts and feeling is erratic, freakish and fitful. When you allow yourself to become irritable, watch how you breathe and you will learn a valuable lesson. Watch how you breathe when you are happy. Watch your breathing when you harbor hate. Watch how you breathe when you feel in love with the whole world and noble emotions thrill you. When filled with good thoughts, you breathe a plentiful supply of oxygen into your lungs and love fills your soul. Love develops a person, physically, mentally and socially. Breathe deeply when you are happy and you will gain life and strength; you will steady your mind and you will develop your power of concentration and become magnetic and powerful.

If you want to get more out of life you must think more of love. Unless you have real affection for something, you have no sentiment, no sweetness, no magnetism. So arouse your love affections by your will and enter into a fuller life.

The hand of love always magnetizes, but it must be steady and controlled. Love can be concentrated in your hand shake, and this is one of the best ways to influence another.

The next time you feel yourself becoming irritable, use your will and be patient. This is a very good exercise in self-control. It will help you to keep patient if you will breathe slowly and deeply. If you find you are commencing to speak fast, just control yourself and speak slowly and clearly. Keep from either raising or lowering your voice and concentrate on the fact that you are determined to keep your poise, and you will improve your power of concentration.

When you meet people of some consequence, assume a reposeful attitude before them. Do this at all times. Watch both them and yourself. Static exercises develop the motor faculties and increase the power of concentration. If you feel yourself getting irritable, nervous or weak, stand squarely on your feet with your chest up and inhale deeply and you will see that your irritability will disappear and a silent calm will pass over you.

If you are in the habit of associating with nervous, irritable people, quit it until you grow strong in the power of concentration, because irritable, angry, fretful, dogmatic and disagreeable people will weaken what powers of resistance you have.

Any exercises that give you better control of the ears, fingers, eyes, feet, help you to steady your mind; when your eye is steady, your mind is steady. One of the best ways to study a person is to watch his physical movements, for, when we study his actions, we are studying his mind. Because actions are the expressions of the mind. As the mind is, so is the action. If it is uneasy, restless, erratic, unsteady, its actions are the same. When it is composed, the mind is composed. Concentration means control of the mind and body. You cannot secure control over one without the other.

Many people who seem to lack ambition have sluggish minds. They are steady, patient and seemingly have good control, but this does not say they are able to concentrate. These people are indolent, inactive, slow and listless, because they lack energy; they do not lose control because they have little force to control. They have no temper and it therefore cannot disturb them. Their actions are steady because they possess little energy. The natural person is internally strong, energetic and forceful, but his energy, force and strength, thoughts and physical movements are well under his control.

If a person does not have energy, both mental and physical, he must develop it. If he has energy which he cannot direct and hold to a point he must learn to do so. A man may be very capable, but, unless he Wills to control his abilities, they will not do him any good.

We hear so much talk about the benefit of physical culture, but the real benefit of this is really lost sight of. There is nothing that holds the faculties at work in a sustained and continuous manner as static exercises do. For, as stated before, when you learn to control the body, you are gaining control over the mind.

# Lesson III: How to Gain What You Want Through Concentration

The ignorant person may say, "How can you get anything by merely wanting it? I say that through concentration you can get anything you want. Every desire can be gratified. But whether it is, will depend upon you concentrating to have that desire fulfilled. Merely wishing for something will not bring it. Wishing you had something shows a weakness and not a belief that you will really get it. So never merely wish, as we are not living in a "fairy age." You use up just as much brain force in "vain imaginings" as you do when you think of something worth while.

Be careful of your desires, make a mental picture of what you want and set your will to this until it materializes. Never allow yourself to drift without helm or rudder. Know what you want to do, and strive with all your might to do it, and you will succeed.

Feel that you can accomplish anything you undertake. Many undertake to do things, but feel when they start they are going to fail and usually they do. I will give an illustration. A man goes to a store for an article. The clerk says, "I am sorry, we have not it." But the man that is determined to get that thing inquires if he doesn't know where he can get it. Again receiving an unsatisfactory answer the determined buyer consults the manager and finally he finds where the article can be bought.

That is the whole secret of concentrating on getting what you want. And, remember, your soul is a center of all-power, and you can accomplish what you will to. "I'll find a way or make one!" is the spirit that wins. I know a man that is now head of a large bank. He started there as a messenger boy. His father had a button made for him with a "P" on it and put it on his coat. He said, "Son, that 'P' is a reminder that some day you are to be the president of your bank. I want you to keep this thought in your mind. Every day do something that will put you nearer your goal." Each night after supper he would say, "Son, what did you do today?" In this way the thought was always kept in mind. He concentrated on becoming president of that bank, and he did. His father told him never to tell anyone what that "P" stood for. A good deal of fun was made of it by his associates. And they tried to find out what it stood for, but they never did until he was made president and then he told the secret.

Don't waste your mental powers in wishes. Don't dissipate your energies by trying to satisfy every whim. Concentrate on doing something really worth while. The man that sticks to something is not the man that fails.

"Power to him who power exerts."—Emerson.

Success to-day depends largely on concentrating on the Interior law of force, for when you do this you awaken those thought powers or forces, which, when used in business, insures permanent results.

Until you are able to do this you have not reached your limit in the use of your forces. This great universe is interwoven with myriads of forces. You make your own place, and whether it is important depends upon you. Through the Indestructible and Unconquerable Law you can in time accomplish all right things and therefore do not be afraid to undertake whatever you really desire to accomplish and are willing to pay for in effort. Anything that is right is possible. That which is necessary will inevitably take place. If something is right it is your duty to do it, though the whole world thinks it to be wrong. "God and one are always a majority," or in plain words, that omnipotent interior law which is God, and the organism that represents you is able to conquer the whole world if your cause is absolutely just. Don't say I wish I was a great man. You can do anything that is proper and you want to do. Just say: You can. You will. You must. Just realize this and the rest is easy. You have the latent faculties and forces to subdue anything that tries to interfere with your plans.

"Let-the-troubles-and-responsibilities-of-life-come-thick-and-fas t. I-am-ready-for-them. My-soul-is-unconquerable. I-represent-the-Infinite-law-of-force,-or-of-all-power. This-God-within-is-my-all-sufficient-strength-and-ever-present-help-in-time-of-trouble. The-more-difficulties-the-greater-its-triumphs-through-me. The-harder-my-trials,-the-faster-I-go-in-the-development-of-my-in herent-strength. Let-all-else-fail-me. This-interior-reliance-is-all-sufficient. The-right-must-prevail. I-demand-wisdom-and-power-to-know-and-follow-the-right. My-higher-self-is-all-wise. I-now-draw-nearer-to-it."

# Lesson IV: Concentration, the Silent Force That Produces Results in All Business

I want you first to realize how powerful thought is. A thought of fear has turned a person's hair gray in a night. A prisoner condemned to die was told that if he would consent to an experiment and lived through it he would be freed. He consented. They wanted to see how much blood a person could lose and still live. They arranged that blood would apparently drop from a cut made in his leg. The cut made was very slight, from which practically no blood escaped. The room was darkened, and the prisoner thought the dropping he heard was really coming from his leg. The next morning he was dead through mental fear.

The two above illustrations will give you a little idea of the power of thought. To thoroughly realize the power of thought is worth a great deal to you.

Through concentrated thought power you can make yourself whatever you please. By thought you can greatly increase your efficiency and strength. You are surrounded by all kinds of thoughts, some good, others bad, and you are sure to absorb some of the latter if you do not build up a positive mental attitude.

If you will study the needless moods of anxiety, worry, despondency, discouragement and others that are the result of uncontrolled thoughts, you will realize how important the control of your thoughts are. Your thoughts make you what you are.

When I walk along the street and study the different people's faces I can tell how they spent their lives. It all shows in their faces, just like a mirror reflects their physical countenances. In looking in those faces I cannot help thinking how most of the people you see have wasted their lives.

The understanding of the power of thought will awaken possibilities within you that you never dreamed of. Never forget that your thoughts are making your environment, your friends, and as your thoughts change these will also. Is this not a practical lesson to learn? Good thoughts are constructive. Evil thoughts are destructive. The desire to do right carries with it a great power. I want you to thoroughly realize the importance of your thoughts, and how to make them valuable, to understand that your thoughts come to you over invisible wires and influence you.

If your thoughts are of a high nature, you become connected with people of the same mental caliber and you are able to help yourself. If your thoughts are tricky, you will bring tricky people to deal with you, who will try to cheat you.

If your thoughts are right kind, you will inspire confidence in those with whom you are dealing.

As you gain the good will of others your confidence and strength will increase. You will soon learn the wonderful value of your thoughts and how serene you can become even when circumstances are the most trying.

Such thoughts of Right and Good Will bring you into harmony with people that amount to something in the world and that are able to give you help if you should need it, as nearly everyone does at times.

You can now see why it is so important to concentrate your thoughts in the proper channels. It is very necessary that people should have confidence in you. When two people meet they have not the time to look each other up. They accept each other according to instinct which can usually be relied on.

You meet a person and his attitude creates a suspicion in you. The chances are you cannot tell why, but something tells you, "Have no dealings with him, for if you do, you will be sorry." Thoughts produce actions. Therefore be careful of your thoughts. Your life will be molded by the thoughts you have. A spiritual power is always available to your thought, and when you are worthy you can attract all the good things without a great effort on your part.

The sun's rays shine down on our gardens, but we can plant trees that will interfere with the sun light. There are invisible forces ready to help you if you do not think and act to intercept these. These forces work silently. "You reap what you sow."

You have concentrated within powers that if developed will bring you happiness greater than you can even imagine. Most people go rushing through life, literally driving away the very things they seek. By concentration you can revolutionize your life, accomplish infinitely more and without a great effort.

Look within yourself and you will find the greatest machine ever made.

How to Speak Wisely. In order to speak wisely you must secure at least a partial concentration of the faculties and forces upon the subject at hand. Speech interferes with the focusing powers of the mind, as it withdraws the attention to the external and therefore is hardly to be compared with that deep silence of the subconscious mind, where deep thoughts, and the silent forces of high potency are evolved. It is necessary to be silent before you can speak wisely. The person that is really alert and well poised and able to speak wisely under trying circumstances, is the person that has practiced in the silence. Most people do not know what the silence is and think it is easy to go into the silence, but this is not so. In the real silence we become attached to that interior law and the forces become silent, because they are in a state of high potency, or beyond the vibratory sounds to which our external ears are attuned. He who desires to become above the ordinary should open up for himself the interior channels which lead to the absolute law of the omnipotent. You can only do this by persistently and intelligently practicing thought concentration. Hold the thought:

In-silence-I-will-allow-my-higher-self-to-have-complete-control. I - w i l l - b e - t r u e - t o - m y - h i g h e r - s e l f . I-will-live-true-to-my-conception-of-what-is-right. I-realize-that-it-is-to-my-self-interest-to-live-up-to-my-best. I-demand-wisdom-so that-I-may-act-wisely-for-myself-and-others.

In the next chapter I will tell you of the mysterious law, which links all humanity together, by the powers of co-operative thought, and chooses for us companionship and friends.

# Lesson V: How Concentrated Thought
# Links All Humanity Together

It is within your power to gratify your every wish. Success is the result of the way you think. I will show you how to think to be successful.

The power to rule and attract success is within yourself. The barriers that shut these off from you are subject to your control. You have unlimited power to think and this is the link that connects you with your omniscient source.

Success is the result of certain moods of mind or ways of thinking. These moods can be controlled by you and produced at will.

You have been evolved to what you are from a lowly atom because you possessed the power to think. This power will never leave you, but will keep urging you on until you reach perfection. As you evolve, you create new desires and these can be gratified. The power to rule lies within you. The barriers that keep you from ruling are also within you. These are the barriers of ignorance.

Concentrated thought will accomplish seemingly impossible results and make you realize your fondest ambitions. At the same time that you break down barriers of limitation new ambitions will be awakened. You begin to experience conscious thought constructions.

If you will just realize that through deep concentration you become linked with thoughts of omnipotence, you will kill out entirely your belief in your limitations and at the same time will drive away all fear and other negative and destructive thought forces which constantly work against you. In the place of these you will build up a strong assurance that your every venture will be successful. When you learn thus how to concentrate and reinforce your thought, you control your mental creations; they in turn help to mould your physical environment, and you become the master of circumstances and the ruler of your kingdom.

It is just as easy to surround your life with what you want as it is with what you don't want. It is a question to be decided by your will. There are no walls to prevent you from getting what you want, providing you want what is right. If you choose something that is not right, you are in opposition to the omnipotent plans of the universe and deserve to fail. But, if you will base your desires on justice and good will, you avail yourself of the helpful powers of universal currents, and instead of having a handicap to work against, can depend upon ultimate success, though the outward appearances may not at first be bright.

Never stop to think of temporary appearances, but maintain an unfaltering belief in your ultimate success. Make your plans carefully, and see that they are not contrary to the tides of universal justice. The main thing for you to remember is to keep at bay the destructive and opposing forces of fear and anger and their satellites.

There is no power so great as the belief which comes from the knowledge that your thought is in harmony with the divine laws of thought and the sincere conviction that your cause is right. You may be able seemingly to accomplish results for a time even if your cause is unjust, but the results will be temporary, and, in time, you will have to tear down your thought edifice and build on the true foundation of Right.

Plans that are not built on truth produce discordant vibrations and are therefore self-destructive. Never try to build until you can build right. It is a waste of time to do anything else. You may temporarily put aside your desire to do right, but its true vibrations will interfere with your unjust plans until you are forced back into righteous paths of power.

All just causes succeed in time, though temporarily they may fail. So if you should face the time when everything seems against you, quiet your fears, drive away all destructive thoughts and uphold the dignity of your moral and spiritual life.

"Where There Is A Will There Is A Way." The reason this is so is that the Will can make a way if given the chance to secure the assistance of aiding forces. The more it is developed the higher the way to which it will lead.

When everything looks gloomy and discouraging, then is the time to show what you are made of by rejoicing that you can control your moods by making them as calm, serene and bright as if prosperity were yours.

"Be faithful in sowing the thought seeds of success, in perfect trust that the sun will not cease to shine and bring a generous harvest in one season."

It is not always necessary to think of the success of a venture when you are actually engaged in it. For when the body is inactive the mind is most free to catch new ideas that will further the opportunity you are seeking. When you are actually engaged in doing something, you are thinking in the channels you have previously constructed and the work does not have to be done over again.

When you are in a negative mood the intuitions are more active, for you are not then controlling your thoughts by the will. Everything we do. should have the approval of the intuition.

When you are in a negative mood you attract thoughts of similar nature through the law of affinity. That is why it is so important to form thoughts of a success nature to attract similar ones. If you have never made a study of this subject, you may think this is all foolishness, but it is a fact that there are thought currents that unerringly bring thoughts of a similar nature. Many persons who think of failure actually attract failure by their worries, their anxieties, their overactivity. These thoughts are bound to bring failure. When you once learn the laws of thought and think of nothing but Good, Truth, Success, you will make more progress with less effort than you ever made before.

There are forces that can aid the mind that are hardly dreamed of by the average person. When you learn to believe more in the value of thought and its laws you will be led aright and your business gains will multiply.

The following method may assist you in gaining better thought control. If you are unable to control your fears, just say to your faulty determination, "Do not falter or be afraid, for I am not really alone. I am surrounded by invisible forces that will assist me to remove the unfavorable appearances." Soon you will have more courage. The only difference between the fearless man and the fearful one is in his will, his hope. So if you lack success, believe in it, hope for it, claim it. You can use the same method to brace up your thoughts of desire, aspiration, imagination, expectation, ambition, understanding, trust and assurance.

If you get anxious, angry, discouraged, undecided or worried, it is because you are not receiving the co-operation of the higher powers of your mind. By your Will you can so organize the powers of the mind that your moods change only as you want them to instead of as circumstances affect you.

I was recently asked if I advised concentrating on what you eat, or what you see while walking. My reply was that no matter what you may be doing, when in practice think of nothing else but that act at the time. The idea is to be able to control your unimportant acts, otherwise you set up a habit that it will be hard to overcome, because your faculties have not been in the habit of concentrating. Your faculties cannot be disorganized one minute and organized the next. If you allow the mind to wander while you are doing small things, it will be likely to get into mischief and make it hard to concentrate on the important act when it comes.

The man that is able to concentrate is the happy, busy man. Time does not drag with him. He always has plenty to do. He does not have time to think over past mistakes, which would make him unhappy.

If despite our discouragement and failures, we claim our great heritage, "life and truth and force, like an electric current," will permeate our lives until we enter into our "birthright in eternity."

The will does not act with clearness, decision and promptness unless it is trained to do so. There are comparatively few that really know what they are doing every minute of the day. This is because they do not observe with sufficient orderliness and accuracy to know what they are doing. It is not difficult to know what you us doing all the time, if you will just practice concentration and with a reposeful deliberation, and train yourself to think clearly, promptly, and decisive. If you allow yourself to worry or hurry in what you are doing, this will not be clearly photographed upon the sensitized plate of the subjective mind, and you therefore will not be really conscious of your actions. So practice accuracy and concentration of thought, and also absolute truthfulness and you will soon be able to concentrate.

# Lesson VI: the Training of the Will to do

The Will To Do is the greatest power in the world that is concerned with human accomplishment and no one can in advance determine its limits.

The things that we do now would have been a few ages ago impossibilities. Today the safe maxim is: "All things are possible."

The Will To Do is a force that is strictly practical, yet it is difficult to explain just what it is. It can be compared to electricity because we know it only through its cause and effects. It is a power we can direct and to just the extent we direct it do we determine our future. Every time you accomplish any definite act, consciously or unconsciously, you use the principle of the Will. You can Will to do anything whether it is right or wrong, and therefore the way you use your will makes a big difference in your life.

Every person possesses some "Will To Do." It is the inner energy which controls all conscious acts. What you will to do directs your life forces. All habits, good or bad, are the result of what you will to do. You improve or lower your condition in life by what you will to do. Your will has a connection with all avenues of knowledge, all activities, all accomplishment.

You probably know of cases where people have shown wonderful strength under some excitement, similar to the following: The house of a farmer's wife caught on fire. No one was around to help her move anything. She was a frail woman, and ordinarily was considered weak. On this occasion she removed things from the house that it later took three men to handle. It was the "Will To Do" that she used to accomplish her task.

Genius Is But A Will To Do Little Things With Infinite Pains. Little Things Well Done Open The Door Of Opportunity For Bigger Things.

The Will accomplishes its greater results through activities that grow out of great concentration in acquiring the power of voluntary attention to such an extent that we can direct it where we will and hold it steadily to its task until our aim is accomplished. When you learn so to use it, your Will Power becomes a mighty force. Almost everything can be accomplished through its proper use. It is greater than physical force because it can be used to control not only physical but mental and moral forces.

There are very few that possess perfectly developed and balanced Will Power, but those who do easily crush out their weak qualities. Study yourself carefully. Find out your greatest weakness and then use your will power to overcome it. In this way eradicate your faults, one by one, until you have built up a strong character and personality.

Rules for Improvement. A desire arises. Now think whether this would be good for you. If it is not, use your Will Power to kill out the desire, but, on the other hand, if it is a righteous desire, summon all your Will Power to your aid, crush all obstacles that confront you and secure possession of the coveted Good.

Slowness in Making Decisions. This is a weakness of Will Power. You know you should do something, but you delay doing it through lack of decision. It is easier not to do a certain thing than to do it, but conscience says to do it. The vast majority of persons are failures because of the lack of deciding to do a thing when it should be done. Those that are successful have been quick to grasp opportunities by making a quick decision. This power of will can be used to bring culture, wealth and health.

Some Special Pointers. For the next week try to make quicker decisions in your little daily affairs. Set the hour you wish to get up and arise exactly at the fixed time. Anything that you should accomplish, do on or ahead of time. You want, of course, to give due deliberation to weighty matters, but by making quick decisions on little things you will acquire the ability to make quick decisions in bigger things. Never procrastinate. Decide quickly one way or the other even at the risk of deciding wrong. Practice this for a week or two and notice your improvement.

The Lack of Initiative. This, too, keeps many men from succeeding. They have fallen into the way of imitating others in all that they do. Very often we hear the expression, "He seems clever enough, but he lacks initiative." Life for them is one continuous grind. Day after day they go through the same monotonous round of duties, while those that are "getting along" are using their initiative to get greater fullness of life. There is nothing so responsible for poverty as this lack of initiative, this power to think and do for ourselves.

You Are as Good as Anyone. You have will power, and if you use it, you will get your share of the luxuries of life. So use it to claim your own. Don't depend on anyone else to help you. We have to fight our own battles. All the world loves a fighter, while the coward is despised by all.

Every person's problems are different, so I can only say "analyze your opportunities and conditions and study your natural abilities." Form plans for improvement and then put them into operation. Now, as I said before, don't just say, "I am going to do so and so," but carry your plan into execution. Don't make an indefinite plan, but a definite one, and then don't give up until your object has been accomplished. Put these suggestions into practice with true earnestness, and you will soon note astonishing results, and your whole life will be completely changed. An excellent motto for one of pure motives is: Through my will power I dare do what I want to. You will find this affirmation has a very strengthening effect.

The Spirit of Perseverance. The spirit of "sticktoitiveness" is the one that wins. Many go just so far and then give up, whereas, if they had persevered a little longer, they would have won out. Many have much initiative, but instead of concentrating it into one channel, they diffuse it through several, thereby dissipating it to such an extent that its effect is lost.

Develop more determination, which is only the Will To Do, and when you start out to do something stick to it until you get results. Of course, before starting anything you must look ahead and see what the "finish leads to." You must select a road that will lead to "somewhere," rather than "nowhere." The journey must be productive of some kind of substantial results. The trouble with so many young men is that they launch enterprises without any end in sight. It is not so much the start as the finish of a journey that counts. Each little move should bring you nearer the goal which you planned to reach before the enterprise began.

Lack of Perseverance is nothing but the lack of the Will To Do. It takes the same energy to say, "I will continue," as to say, "I give up." Just the moment you say the latter you shut off your dynamo, and your determination is gone. Every time you allow your determination to be broken you weaken it. Don't forget this. Just the instant you notice your determination beginning to weaken, concentrate on it and by sheer Will Power make it continue on the "job."

Never try to make a decision when you are not in a calm state of mind. If in a "quick temper," you are likely to say things you afterwards regret. In anger, you follow impulse rather than reason. No one can expect to achieve success if he makes decisions when not in full control of his mental forces.

Therefore make it a fixed rule to make decisions only when at your best. If you have a "quick temper," you can quickly gain control over it by simple rule of counting backwards. To count backwards requires concentration, and you thus quickly regain a calm state. In this way you can break the "temper habit."

It will do you a lot of good to think over what you said and thought the last time you were angry. Persevere until you see yourself as others see you. It would do no harm to write the scene out in story form and then sit in judgment of the character that played your part.

Special Instructions to Develop the Will To Do. This is a form of mental energy, but requires the proper mental attitude to make it manifest. We hear of people having wonderful will power, which really is wrong. It should be said that they use their will power while with many it is a latent force. I want you to realize that no one has a monopoly on will power. There is plenty for all. What we speak of as will power is but the gathering together of mental energy, the concentration power at one point. So never think of that person as having a stronger will than yours. Each person will be supplied with just that amount of will power that he demands. You don't have to develop will power if you constantly make use of all you have, and remember the way in which you use it determines your fate, for your life is moulded to great extent by the use you make of your will. Unless you make proper use of it you have neither independence nor firmness. You are unable to control yourself and become a mere machine for others to use. It is more important to learn to use your will than to develop your intellect. The man that has not learned how to use his will rarely decides things for himself, but allows his resolutions to be changed by others. He fluctuates from one opinion to another, and of course does not accomplish anything out of the ordinary, while his brother with the trained will takes his place among the world's leaders.

# Lesson VII: The Concentrated Mental Demand

The Mental Demand is the potent force in achievement. The attitude of the mind affects the expression of the face, determines action, changes our physical condition and regulates our lives.

I will not here attempt to explain the silent force that achieves results. You want to develop your mental powers so you can effect the thing sought, and that is what I want to teach you. There is wonderful power and possibility in the concentrated Mental Demand. This, like all other forces, is controlled by laws. It can, like all other forces, be wonderfully increased by consecutive, systematized effort.

The mental demand must be directed by every power of the mind and every possible element should be used to make the demand materialize. You can so intently desire a thing that you can exclude all distracting thoughts. When you practice this singleness of concentration until you attain the end sought, you have developed a Will capable of accomplishing whatever you wish.

As long as you can only do the ordinary things you will be counted in the mass of mediocrity. But just as quick as you surpass others by even comparatively small measure, you are classed as one of life's successes. So, if you wish to emerge into prominence, you must accomplish something more than the ordinary man or woman. It is easy to do this if you will but concentrate on what you desire, and put forth your best effort. It is not the runner with the longest legs or the strongest muscles that wins the race, but the one that can put forth the greatest desire force. You can best understand this by thinking of an engine. The engine starts up slowly, the engineer gradually extending the throttle to the top notch. It is then keyed up to its maximum speed. The same is true of two runners. They start off together and gradually they increase their desire to go faster. The one that has the greatest intensity of desire will win. He may outdistance the other by only a fraction of an inch, yet he gets the laurels.

The men that are looked upon as the world's successes have not always been men of great physical power, nor at the start did they seem very well adapted to the conditions which encompassed them. In the beginning they were not considered men of superior genius, but they won their success by their resolution to achieve results in their undertakings by permitting no set-back to dishearten them; no difficulties to daunt them. Nothing could turn them or influence them against their determination. They never lost sight of their goal. In all of us there is this silent force of wonderful power. If developed, it can overcome conditions that would seem insurmountable. It is constantly urging us on to greater achievement. The more we become acquainted with it the better strategists we become, the more courage we develop and the greater the desire within us for self-expression in activity along many lines.

No one will ever be a failure if he becomes conscious of this silent force within that controls his destiny. But without the consciousness of this inner force, you will not have a clear vision, and external conditions will not yield to the power of your mind. It is the mental resolve that makes achievement possible. Once this has been formed it should never be allowed to cease to press its claim until its object is attained. To make plans work out it will, at times, be necessary to use every power of your mind. Patience, perseverance and all the indomitable forces within one will have to be mustered and used with the greatest effectiveness.

Perseverance is the first element of success. In order to persevere you must be ceaseless in your application. It requires you to concentrate your thoughts upon your undertaking and bring every energy to bear upon keeping them focused upon it until you have accomplished your aim. To quit short of this is to weaken all future efforts.

The Mental Demand seems an unreal power because it is intangible; but it is the mightiest power in the world. It is a power that is free for you to use. No one can use it for you. The Mental Demand is not a visionary one. It is a potent force, which you can use freely without cost. When you are in doubt it will counsel you. It will guide you when you are uncertain. When you are in fear it will give you courage. It is the motive power which supplies the energies necessary to the achievement of the purpose. You have a large store house of possibilities. The Mental Demand makes possibilities realities. It supplies everything necessary for the accomplishment, It selects the tools and instructs how to use them. It makes you understand the situation. Every time you make a Mental Demand you strengthen the brain centers by drawing to you external forces.

Few realize the power of a Mental Demand. It is possible to make your demand so strong that you can impart what you have to say to another without speaking to him. Have you ever, after planning to discuss a certain matter with a friend, had the experience of having him broach the subject before you had a chance to speak of it? Have you ever, in a letter, made a suggestion to a friend that he carried out before your letter reached him? Have you ever wanted to speak to a person who, just then walked in or telephoned. I have had many such responses to thought and you and your friends have doubtless experienced them, too.

These two things are neither coincidences nor accidents, but are the results of mental demand launched by strong concentration.

The person that never wants anything gets little. To demand resolutely is the first step toward getting what you want.

The power of the Mental Demand seems absolute, the supply illimitable. The mental demand projects itself and causes to materialize the conditions and opportunities needed to accomplish the purpose. Do not think I over estimate the value of the Mental Demand. It brings the fuller life if used for only righteous purposes. Once the Mental Demand is made, however, never let it falter. If you do the current that connects you with your desire is broken. Take all the necessary time to build a firm foundation, so that there need not be even an element of doubt to creep in. Just the moment you entertain "doubt" you lose some of the demand force, and force once lost is hard to regain. So whenever you make a mental demand hold steadfastly to it until your need is supplied.

I want to repeat again that Power of Mental Demand is not a visionary one. It is concentrated power only, and can be used by you. It is not supernatural power, but requires a development of the brain centers. The outcome is sure when it is given with a strong resolute determination.

No person will advance to any great extent, until he recognizes this force within him. If you have not become aware of it, you have not made very much of a success of your life. It is this "something" that distinguishes that "man" from other men. It is this subtle power that develops strong personality.

If you want a great deal you must demand a great deal. Once you make your demand, anticipate its fulfillment. It depends upon us. We are rewarded according to our efforts. The Power of Mental Demand can bring us what we want. We become what we determine to be. We control our own destiny.

Get the right mental attitude, then in accordance with your ability you can gain success.

And every man of *average* ability, the ordinary man that you see about you, can be really successful, independent, free of worry, *his own master*, if he can manage to do just two things.

First, remain forever dissatisfied with what he *is* doing and with what he *has* accomplished.

Second, develop in his mind a belief that the word impossible was not intended or him. Build up in his mind the confidence that enables the mind to use its power.

Many, especially the older men, will ask:

"How can I build up that self-confidence in my brain? How can I, after months and years of discouragement, of dull plodding, suddenly conceive and carry out a plan for doing something that will mike life worth while and change the monotonous routine?

"How can a man get out of a rut after he has been in it for years and has settled down to the slow jog-trot that leads to the grave?"

The answer is the thing can be done, and millions have done it.

One of the names most honored among the great men of France is that of Littre, who wrote and compiled the great French dictionary—a monument of learning. He is the man whose place among the forty immortals of France was taken by the great Pasteur, when the latter was elected to the Academy.

Littre *began* the work that makes him famous when he was more than sixty years old.

## Lesson VIII: Concentration Gives Mental Poise

You will find that the man that concentrates is well poised, whereas the man that allows his mind to wander is easily upset. When in this state wisdom does not pass from the subconscious storehouse into the consciousness. There must be mental quiet before the two consciousnesses can work in harmony. When you are able to concentrate you have peace of mind.

If you are in the habit of losing your poise, form the habit of reading literature that has a quieting power. Just the second you feel your poise slipping, say, "Peace," and then hold this thought in mind and you will never lose your self-control.

There cannot be perfect concentration until there is peace of mind. So keep thinking peace, acting peace, until you are at peace with all the world. For when once you have reached this state there will be no trouble to concentrate on anything you wish.

When you have peace of mind you are not timid or anxious, or fearful, or rigid and you will not allow any disturbing thought to influence you. You cast aside all fears, and think of yourself as a spark of the Divine Being, as a manifestation of the "One Universal Principle" that fills all space and time. Think of yourself thus as a child of the infinite, possessing infinite possibilities.

Write on a piece of paper, "I have the power to do and to be whatever I wish to do and be." Keep this mentally before you, and you will find the thought will be of great help to you.

The Mistake of Concentrating on Your Business While Away. In order to be successful today, you must concentrate, but don't become a slave to concentration, and carry your business cares home. Just as sure as you do you will be burning the life forces at both ends and the fire will go out much sooner than was intended.

Many men become so absorbed in their business that when they go to church they do not hear the preacher because their minds are on their business. If they go to the theater they do not enjoy it because their business is on their minds. When they go to bed they think about business instead of sleep and wonder why they don't sleep. This is the wrong kind of concentration and is dangerous. It is involuntary. When you are unable to get anything out of your mind it becomes unwholesome as any thought held continuously causes weariness of the flesh. It is a big mistake to let a thought rule you, instead of ruling it. He who does not rule himself is not a success. If you cannot control your concentration, your health will suffer.

So never become so absorbed with anything that you cannot lay it aside and take up another. This is self-control.

Concentration Is Paying Attention to a Chosen Thought. Everything that passes before the eye makes an impression on the subconscious mind, but unless you pay attention to some certain thing you will not remember what you saw. For instance if you walked down a busy street without seeing anything that attracted your particular attention, you could not recall anything you saw. So you see only what attracts your attention. If you work you only see and remember what you think about. When you concentrate on something it absorbs your whole thought.

Self-Study Valuable. Everyone has some habits that can be overcome by concentration. We will say for instance, you are in the habit of complaining, or finding fault with yourself or others; or, imagining that you do not possess the ability of others; or feeling that you are not as good as someone else; or that you cannot rely on yourself; or harboring any similar thoughts or thoughts of weakness. These should be cast aside and instead thoughts of strength should be put in their place. Just remember every time you think of yourself as being weak, in some way you are making yourself so by thinking you are. Our mental conditions make us what we are. Just watch yourself and see how much time you waste in worrying, fretting and complaining. The more of it you do the worse off you are.

Just the minute you are aware of thinking a negative thought immediately change to a positive one. If you start to think of failure, change to thinking of success. You have the germ of success within you. Care for it the same as the setting hen broods over the eggs and you can make it a reality.

You can make those that you come in contact with feel as you do, because you radiate vibrations of the way you feel and your vibrations are felt by others. When you concentrate on a certain thing you turn all the rays of your vibrations on this. Thought is the directing power of all Life's vibrations. If a person should enter a room with a lot of people and feel as if he were a person of no consequence no one would know he was there unless they saw him, and even if they did, they would not remember seeing him, because they were not attracted towards him. But let him enter the room feeling that he was magnetic and concentrating on this thought, others would feel his vibration. So remember the way you feel you can make others feel. This is the law.

146 William Walker Atkinson

Make yourself a concentrated dynamo from which your thoughts vibrate to others. Then you are a power in the world. Cultivate the art of feeling, for as I said before you can only make others feel what you feel.

If you will study all of the great characters of history you will find that they were enthusiastic. First they were enthusiastic themselves, and then they could arouse others' enthusiasm. It is latent in everyone. It is a wonderful force when once aroused. All public men to be a success have to possess it. Cultivate it by concentration. Set aside some hour of the day, wherein to hold rapt converse with the soul. Meditate with sincere desire and contrite heart and you will be able to accomplish that which you have meditated on. This is the keynote of success.

"Think, speak and act just as you wish to be, And you will be that which you wish to be."

You are just what you think you are and not what you may appear to be. You may fool others but not yourself. You may control your life and actions just as you can control your hands. If you want to raise your hand you must first think of raising it. If you want to control your life you must first control your thinking. Easy to do, is it not? Yes it is, if you will but concentrate on what you think about.

For he only can  That says he will.

How can we secure concentration? To this question, the first and last answer must be: By interest and strong motive. The stronger the motive the greater the concentration.—Eustace Miller, M. D.

The Successful Lives Are the Concentrated Lives. The utterly helpless multitude that sooner or later have to be cared for by charity, are those that were never able to concentrate, and who have become the victims of negative ideas.

Train yourself so you will be able to centralize your thought and develop your brain power, and increase your mental energy, or you can be a slacker, a drifter, a quitter or a sleeper. It all depends on how you concentrate, or centralize your thoughts. Your thinking then becomes a fixed power and you do not waste time thinking about something that would not be good for you. You pick out the thoughts that will be the means of bringing you what you desire, and they become a material reality. Whatever we create in the thought world will some day materialize. That is the law. Don't forget this.

In the old days men drifted without concentration but this is a day of efficiency and therefore all of our efforts must be concentrated, if we are to win any success worth the name.

Why People Often Do Not Get What They Concentrate On. Because they sit down in hopeless despair and expect it to come to them. But if they will just reach out for it with their biggest effort they will find it is within their reach. No one limits us but ourselves. We are what we are today as the result of internal conditions. We can control the external conditions. They are subject to our will.

Through our concentration we can attract what we want, because we became enrapport with the Universal forces, from which we can get what we want.

You have watched races no doubt. They all line up together. Each has his mind set on getting to the goal before the others. This is one kind of concentration. A man starts to think on a certain subject. He has all kinds of thoughts come to him, but by concentration he shuts out all these but the one he has chosen. Concentration is just a case of willing to do a certain thing and doing it.

If you want to accomplish anything first put yourself in a concentrating, reposeful, receptive, acquiring frame of mind. In tackling unfamiliar work make haste slowly and deliberately and then you will secure that interior activity, which is never possible when you are in a hurry or under a strain. When you "think hard" or try to hurry results too quickly, you generally shut off the interior flow of thoughts and ideas. You have often no doubt tried hard to think of something but could not, but just as soon as you stopped trying to think of it, it came to you.

# Lesson IX: Concentration Can Overcome Bad Habits

Habits make or break us to a far greater extent than we like to admit. Habit is both a powerful enemy and wonderful ally of concentration. You must learn to overcome habits which are injurious to concentration, and to cultivate those which increase it.

The large majority of people are controlled by their habits and are buffeted around by them like waves of the ocean tossing a piece of wood. They do things in a certain way because of the power of habit. They seldom ever think of concentrating on why they do them this or that way, or study to see if they could do them in a better way. Now my object in this chapter is to get you to concentrate on your habits so you can find out which are good and which are bad for you. You will find that by making a few needed changes you can make even those that are not good for you, of service; the good habits you can make much better.

The first thing I want you to realize is that all habits are governed consciously or unconsciously by the will. Most of us are forming new habits all the time. Very often, if you repeat something several times in the same way, you will have formed the habit of doing it that way. But the oftener you repeat it the stronger that habit grows and the more deeply it becomes embedded in your nature. After a habit has been in force for a long time, it becomes almost a part of you, and is therefore hard to overcome. But you can still break any habit by strong concentration on its opposite.

"All our life, so far as it has definite form, is but a mass of habits—practical, emotional, and intellectual—systematically organized, for our weal or woe, and bearing us irresistibly toward our destiny whatever the latter may be."

We are creatures of habits, "imitators and copiers of our past selves." We are liable to be "bent" or "curved" as we can bend a piece of paper, and each fold leaves a crease, which makes it easier to make the fold there the next time. "The intellect and will are spiritual functions; still they are immersed in matter, and to every movement of theirs, corresponds a movement in the brain, that is, in their material correlative." This is why habits of thought and habits of willing can be formed. All physical impressions are the carrying out of the actions of the will and intellect. Our nervous systems are what they are today, because of the way they have been exercised.

As we grow older most of us become more and more like automatic machines. The habits we have formed increase in strength. We work in our old characteristic way. Your associates learn to expect you to do things in a certain way. So you see that your habits make a great difference in your life, and as it is just about as easy to form good habits as it is bad, you should form only the former. No one but yourself is responsible for your habits. You are free to form the habits that you should and if everyone could realize the importance of forming the right kind of habits what a different world this would be. How much happier everyone would be. Then all instead of the few might win success.

Habits are formed more quickly when we are young, but if we have already passed the youthful plastic period the time to start to control our habits is right now, as we will never be any younger.

You will find the following maxims worth remembering.

First Maxim:

"We must make our nervous system our ally instead of our enemy."

Second Maxim:

"In the acquisition of a new habit as in the leaving off of an old one, we must take care to launch ourselves with as strong and decided an initiative as possible."

The man that is in the habit of doing the right thing from boyhood, has only good motives, so it is very important for you that you concentrate assiduously on the habits that reinforce good motives. Surround yourself with every aid you can. Don't play with fire by forming bad habits. Make a new beginning today. Study why you have been doing certain things. If they are not for your good, shun them henceforth. Don't give in to a single temptation for every time you do, you strengthen the chain of bad habits. Every time you keep a resolution you break the chain that enslaves you.

Third Maxim:

"Never allow an exception to occur till the new habit is securely rooted in your life." Here is the idea, you never want to give in, until the new habit is fixed else you undo all that has been accomplished by previous efforts. There are two opposing inclinations. One wants to be firm, and the other wants to give in. By your will you can become firm, through repetition. Fortify your will to be able to cope with any and all opposition.

Fourth Maxim:

"Seize the very first possible opportunity to act on every resolution you make, and on every emotional prompting you may experience in the direction of the habits you aspire to gain."

To make a resolve and not to keep it is of little value. So by all means keep every resolution you make, for you not only profit by the resolution, but it furnishes you with an exercise that causes the brain cells and physiological correlatives to form the habit of adjusting themselves to carry out resolutions. "A tendency to act, becomes effectively engrained in us in proportion to the uninterrupted frequency with which the actions actually occur, and the brain 'grows' to their use. When a resolve or a fine glow of feeling is allowed to evaporate without bearing fruit, it is worse than a chance lost."

If you keep your resolutions you form a most valuable habit. If you break them you form a most dangerous one. So concentrate on keeping them, whether important or unimportant, and remember it is just as important for this purpose to keep the unimportant, for by so doing you are forming the habit.

Fifth Maxim:

"Keep the faculty of effort alive in you by a little gratuitous exercise every day."

The more we exercise the will, the better we can control our habits. "Every few days do something for no other reason than its difficulty, so that when the hour of dire need draws nigh, it may find you not unnerved or untrained to stand the test. Asceticism of this sort is like the insurance which a man pays on his house and goods. The tax does him no good at the time, and possibly may never bring him a return, but if the fire does come, his having paid it will be his salvation from ruin. So with the man who has daily insured himself to habits of concentrated attention, energetic volation, and self-denial in unnecessary things. "He will stand like a tower when everything rocks around him and his softer fellow-mortals are winnowed like chaff in the blast."

The young should be made to concentrate on their habits and be made to realize that if they don't they become walking bundles of injurious habits. Youth is the plastic state, and should be utilized in laying the foundation for a glorious future.

The great value of habit for good and evil cannot be overestimated. "Habit is the deepest law of human nature." No man is stronger than his habits, because his habits either build up his strength or decrease it.

Why We Are Creatures of Habits. Habits have often been called a labor-saving invention, because when they are formed they require less of both mental and material strength. The more deeply the habit becomes ingrained the more automatic it becomes. Therefore habit is an economizing tendency of our nature, for if it were not for habit we should have to be more watchful. We walk across a crowded street; the habit of stopping and looking prevents us from being hurt. The right kind of habits keeps us from making mistakes and mishaps. It is a well known fact that a chauffeur is not able to master his machine safely until he has trained his body in a habitual way. When an emergency comes he instantly knows what to do. Where safety depends on quickness the operator must work automatically. Habits mean less risk, less fatigue, and greater accuracy.

"You do not want to become a slave to habits of a trivial nature. For instance, Wagner required a certain costume before he could compose corresponding parts of his operas. Schiller could never write with ease unless there were rotten apples in the drawer of his desk from which he could now and then obtain an odor which seemed to him sweet. Gladstone had different desks for his different activities, so that when he worked on Homer he never sat among habitual accompaniments of his legislative labors."

In order to overcome undesirable habits, two things are necessary. You must have trained your will to do what you want it to do, and the stronger the will the easier it will be to break a habit. Then you must make a resolution to do just the opposite of what the habit is. Therefore one habit must replace another. If you have a strong will, you can tenaciously and persistently concentrate on removing the bad habit and in a very short time the good habit will gain the upper hand. I will bring this chapter to a close by giving Doctor Oppenheim's instructions for overcoming a habit:

"If you want to abolish a habit, and its accumulated circumstances as well, you must grapple with the matter as earnestly as you would with a physical enemy. You must go into the encounter with all tenacity of determination, with all fierceness of resolve—yea, even with a passion for success that may be called vindictive. No human enemy can be as insidious, so persevering, as unrelenting as an unfavorable habit. It never sleeps, it needs no rest.

"It is like a parasite that grows with the growth of the supporting body, and, like a parasite, it can best be killed by violent separation and crushing.

When life is stormy and all seems against us, that is when we often acquire wrong habits, and it is then, that we have to make a gigantic effort to think and speak as we should; and even though we may feel the very reverse at that moment the tiniest effort will be backed up by a tremendous Power and will lift us to a realization never felt before. It is not in the easy, contented moments of our life that we make our greatest progress, for then it requires, no special effort to keep in tune. But it is when we are in the midst of trials and misfortunes, when we think we are sinking, being overwhelmed, then it is important for us to realize that we are linked to a great Power and if we live as we should, there is nothing that can occur in life, which could permanently injure us, nothing can happen that should disturb us. So always remember you have within you unlimited power, ready to manifest itself in the form which fills our need at the moment. If, when we have something difficult to solve, we would be silent like the child, we can get the inspiration when it comes; we will know how to act, we will find there is no need to hurry or disturb ourselves, that it is always wiser to wait for guidance from within, than to act on impulse from Without.

# Lesson X: Business Results Through Concentration

A successful business is not usually the result of chance. Neither is a failure the result of luck. Most failures could be determined in advance if the founders had been studied. It is not always possible to start a money-making business at the start. Usually a number of changes have to be made. Plans do not work out as their creators thought they would. They may have to be changed a little, broadened it may be, here and there, and as you broaden your business you broaden your power to achieve. You gain an intense and sustained desire to make your business a success.

When you start a business you may have but a vague notion of the way you will conduct it. You must fill in the details as you go along. You must concentrate on these details. As you straighten out one after another, others will require attention. In this way you cover the field of "the first endeavor" and new opportunities open up for you.

When you realize one desire, another comes. But if you do not fulfill the first desire, you will not the second. The person that does not carry his desires into action is only a dreamer. Desire is a great creative force, if it is pure, intense and sustained. It is our desires that keep stirring us up to action and they will strengthen and broaden you if you make them materialize.

Every man who achieves success deserves it. When he first started out he did not understand how to solve the problems that afterwards presented themselves, but he did each thing as it came up in the very best way that he could, and this developed his power of doing bigger things. We become masters of business by learning to do well whatever we attempt. The man that has a thorough knowledge of his business can of course direct it much more easily and skillfully than the man who lacks that knowledge. The skilled business director can sit in his private office and still know accurately what is actually being done. He knows what should be done in any given time and if it is not accomplished he knows that his employees are not turning out the work that they should. It is then easy to apply the remedy.

Business success depends on well-concentrated efforts. You must use every mental force you can master. The more these are used the more they increase. Therefore the more you accomplish today the more force you will have at your disposal with which to solve your problems tomorrow.

If you are working for someone else today and wish to start in a business for yourself, think over carefully what you would like to do. Then when you have resolved what you want to do, you will be drawn towards it. There is a law that opens the way to the fulfillment of your desires. Of course back of your desire you must put forward the necessary effort to carry out your purpose; you must use your power to put your desires into force. Once they are created and you keep up your determination to have them fulfilled you both consciously and unconsciously work toward their materialization. Set your heart on your purpose, concentrate your thought upon it, direct your efforts with all your intelligence and in due time you will realize your ambition.

Feel yourself a success, believe you are a success and thus put yourself in the attitude that demands recognition and the thought current draws to you what you need to make you a success. Don't be afraid of big undertakings. Go at them with grit, and pursue methods that you think will accomplish your purpose. You may not at first meet with entire success, but aim so high that if you fall a little short you will still have accomplished much.

What others have done you can do. You may even do what others have been unable to do. Always keep a strong desire to succeed in your mind. Be in love with your aim and work, and make them, as far as possible, square with the rule of the greatest good to the greatest number and your life cannot be a failure.

The successful business attitude must be cultivated to make the most out of your life, the attitude of expecting great things from both yourself and others. It alone will often cause men to make good; to measure up to the best that is in them.

It is not the spasmodic spurts that count on a long journey, but the steady efforts. Spurts fatigue and make it hard for you to continue.

Rely on your own opinion. It should be as good as anyone's else. When once you reach a conclusion abide by it. Let there be no doubt, or wavering in your judgment. If you are uncertain about every decision you make, you will be subject to harassing doubts and fears which will render your judgment of little value. The man that decides according to what he thinks right and who learns from every mistake acquires a well balanced mind that gets the best results. He gains the confidence of others. He is known as the man that knows what he wants, and not as one that is as changeable as the weather. The man of today wants to do business with the man that he can depend upon. Uncertainties in the business world are meeting with more disfavor. Reliable firms want to do business with men of known qualities, with men of firmness, judgment and reliability.

So if you wish to start in business for yourself your greatest asset, with the single exception of a sound physique, is that of a good reputation.

A successful business is not hard to build if we can concentrate all our mental forces upon it. It is the man that is unsettled because he does not know what he wants that goes to the wall. We hear persons say that business is trying on the nerves, but it is the unsettling elements of fret and worry and suspense that are nerve-exhausting and not the business. Executing one's plans may cause fatigue, enjoyment comes with rest. If there has not been any unnatural strain, the recuperative powers replace what energy has been lost.

By attending to each day's work properly you develop the capacity to do a greater work tomorrow. It is this gradual development that makes possible the carrying out of big plans. The man that figures out doing something each hour of the day gets somewhere. At the end of each day you should be a step nearer your aim. Keep the idea in mind, that you mean to go forward, that each day must mark an advance and forward you will go. You do not even have to know the exact direction so long as you are determined to find the way. But you must not turn back once you have started.

Even brilliant men's conceptions of the possibilities of their mental forces are so limited and below their real worth that they are far more likely to belittle their possibilities than they are to exaggerate them. You don't want to think that an aim is impossible because it has never been realized in the past. Every day someone is doing something that was never done before. We are pushing ahead faster. Formerly it took decades to build up a big business, but today it is only but a matter of years, sometimes of months.

Plan each day's activities carefully and you can reach any height you aim at. If each thing you do is done with concise and concentrated thought you will be able to turn out an excellent quality and a large quantity of work. Plan to do so much work during the day and you will be astonished to see how much more you will do, than on other days, when you had not decided on any certain amount. I have demonstrated that the average business working force could do the same amount of work in six hours that they now do in eight, without using up any more energy. Never start to accomplish anything in an indecisive, indefinite, uncertain way. Tackle everything with a positiveness and an earnestness that will concentrate your mind and attract the very best associated thoughts. You will in a short time find that you will have extra time for planning bigger things.

The natural leader always draws to himself, by the law of mental attraction, ideas in his chosen subject that have ever been conceived by others. This is of the greatest importance and help. If you are properly trained you benefit much by others' thoughts, and, providing you generate from within yourself something of value, they will benefit from yours. "We are heirs of all the ages," but we must know how to use our inheritance.

The confident, pushing, hopeful, determined man influences all with whom he associates, and inspires the same qualities in them. You feel that his is a safe example to follow and he rouses the same force within you that is pushing him onward and upward.

One seldom makes a success of anything that he goes at in a listless, spiritless way. To build up a business you must see it expanding in your mind before it actually takes tangible shape. Every great task that has ever been accomplished has first been merely a vision in the mind of its creator. Detail after detail has had to be worked out in his mind from his first faint idea of the enterprise. Finally a clear idea was formed and then the accomplishment, which was only the material result of the mental concept, followed.

The up-to-date business man is not content to build only for the present, but is planning ahead. If he does not he will fall behind his competitor, who is. What we are actually doing today was carefully thought out and planned by others in the past. All progressive businesses are conducted this way. That is why the young business man of today is likely to accomplish more in a few years than his father did in all his life. There is no reason why your work or business should fag you out. When it does there is something wrong. You are attracting forces and influence that you should not, because you are not in harmony with what you are doing. There is nothing so tiring as to try to do the work for which we are unfitted, both by temperament and training.

Each one should be engaged in a business that he loves; be should be furthering movements with which he is in sympathy. He will then only do his best work and take intense pleasure in his business. In this way, while constantly growing and developing his powers, he is at the same time rendering through his work, genuine and devoted service to humanity.

Business success is not the result of chance, but of scientific ideas and plans carried out by an aggressive and progressive management. Use your mental forces so that they will grow and develop. Remember that everything you do is the result of mental action, therefore you can completely control your every action. Nothing is impossible for you. Don't be afraid to tackle a difficult proposition. Your success will depend upon the use you make of your mind. This is capable of wonderful development. See that you make full use of it, and not only develop yourself but your associates. Try to broaden the visions of those with whom you come in contact and you will broaden your own outlook of life.

Are You Afraid of Responsibilities? In order for the individual soul to develop, you must have responsibilities. You must manifest the omnipotence of the law of supply. The whole world is your legitimate sphere of activity. How much of a conqueror are you? What have you done? Are you afraid of responsibility, or are you ever dodging, flinching, or side stepping it. If you are, you are not a Real Man. Your higher self never winces, so be a man and allow the powers of the higher self to manifest and you will find you have plenty of strength and you will feel better when you are tackling difficult propositions.

# Lesson XI: Concentrate on Courage

Courage is the backbone of man. The man with courage has persistence. He states what he believes and puts it into execution. The courageous man has confidence. He draws to himself all the moral qualities and mental forces which go to make up a strong man. Whereas, the man without courage draws to himself all the qualities of a weak man, vacillation, doubt, hesitancy, and unsteadiness of purpose. You can therefore see the value of concentration on courage. It is a most vital element of success.

The lack of courage creates financial, as well as mental and moral difficulties. When a new problem comes, instead of looking upon it as something to be achieved, the man or woman without courage looks for reasons why it cannot be done and failure is naturally the almost inevitable result. This is a subject well worthy of your study. Look upon everything within your power as a possibility instead of as merely a probability and you will accomplish a great deal more, because by considering a thing as impossible, you immediately draw to yourself all the elements that contribute to failure. Lack of courage destroys your confidence in yourself. It destroys that forceful, resolute attitude so important to success.

The man without courage unconsciously draws to himself all that is contemptible, weakening, demoralizing and destructive. He then blames his luck when he does not secure the things he weakly desires. We must first have the courage to strongly desire something. A desire to be fulfilled must be backed by the strength of all our mental forces. Such a desire has enough commanding force to change all unfavorable conditions. The man with courage commands, whether be is on the battlefield or in business life.

What is courage? It is the Will To Do. It takes no more energy to be courageous than to be cowardly. It is a matter of the right training in the right way. Courage concentrates the mental forces on the task at hand. It then directs them thoughtfully, steadily, deliberately, while attracting all the forces of success, toward the desired end. Cowardice on the other hand, dissipates both our mental and moral forces, thereby inviting failure.

As we are creatures of habits, we should avoid persons that lack courage. They are easy to discover because of their habits of fear in attacking new problems. The man with courage is never afraid.

Start out today with the idea that there is no reason why you should not be courageous. If any fear-thoughts come to you cast them off as you would the deadly viper. Form the habit of never thinking of anything unfavorable to yourself or anyone else. In dealing with difficulties, new or old, hold ever the thought, "I am courageous." Whenever a doubt crosses the threshold of your mind, banish it. Remember, you as master of your mind control its every thought, and here is a good one to often affirm, "I have courage because I desire it; because I need it; because I use it and because I refuse to become such a weakling as cowardice produces."

There is no justification for the loss of courage. The evils by which you will almost certainly be overwhelmed without it are far greater than those which courage will help you to meet and overcome. Right, then, must be the moralist who says that the only thing to fear is fear.

Never let another's opinion affect you; he cannot tell what you are able to do; he does not know what you can do with your forces. The truth is you do not know yourself until you put yourself to the test. Therefore, how can someone else know? Never let anyone else put a valuation on you.

Almost all wonderful achievements have been accomplished after it had been "thoroughly" demonstrated that they were impossibilities. Once we understand the law, all things are possible. If they were impossibilities we could not conceive them.

Just the moment you allow someone to influence you against what you think is right, you lose that confidence in yourself that inspires courage and carries with it all the forces which courage creates. Just the moment you begin to swerve in your plan you begin to carry out another's thought and not your own. You become the directed and not the director. You forsake the courage and resolution of your own mind, and you therefore lack the very forces that you need to sustain and carry out your work. Instead of being self-reliant you become timid and this invites failure. When you permit yourself to be influenced from your plan by another, you are unable to judge as you should, because you have allowed another's influence to deprive you of your courage and determination without absorbing any of his in return so you are in much the same predicament, as you would be in if you turned over all your worldly possessions to another without getting "value received."

Concentrate on just the opposite of fear, want, poverty, sickness, etc. Never doubt your own ability. You have plenty, if you will just use it. A great many men are failures because they doubt their own capacity. Instead of building up strong mental forces which would be of the greatest use to them their fear thoughts tear them down. Fear paralyzes energy. It keeps us from attracting the forces that go to make up success. Fear is the worst enemy we have.

There are few people that really know that they can accomplish much. They desire the full extent of their powers, but alas, it is only occasionally that you find a man that is aware of the great possibilities within him. When you believe with all your mind and heart and soul that you can do something, you thereby develop the courage to steadily and confidently live up to that belief. You have now gone a long way towards accomplishing it. The chances are that there will be obstacles, big and little, in your way, but resolute courage will overcome them and nothing else will. Strong courage eliminates the injurious and opposing forces by summoning their masters, the yet stronger forces that will serve you.

Courage is yours for the asking. All you have to do is to believe in it, claim it and use it. To succeed in business believe that it will be successful, assert that it is successful, and work like a beaver to make it so. Difficulties soon melt away before the courageous. One man of courage can fire with his spirit a whole army of men, whether it be military or industrial, because courage, like cowardice, is contagious.

The man of courage overcomes the trials and temptations of life; he commands success; he renders sound judgment; he develops personal influence and a forceful character and often becomes the mentor of the community which he serves.

How to Overcome Depression and Melancholia. Both of the former are harmful and make you unhappy. These are states that can be quickly overcome through concentrating more closely on the higher self, for when you do you cut off the connection with the harmful force currents. You can also drive away moods by simply choosing and fully concentrating on an agreeable subject. Through will power and thought control we can accomplish anything we want to do. There is wonderful inherent power within us all, and there is never any sufficient cause for fear, except ignorance.

Every evil is but the product of ignorance, and everyone that possesses the power to think has the power to overcome ignorance and evil. The pain that we suffer from doing evil are but the lessons of experience, and the object of the pain is to make us realize our ignorance. When we become depressed It is evidence that our thought faculties are combining improperly and thereby attracting the wrong force-currents.

All that it is necessary to do is to exercise the will and concentrate upon happy subjects. I will only think of subjects worthy of my higher self and its powers.

# Lesson XII: Concentrate on Wealth

It was never intended that man should be poor. When wealth is obtained under the proper conditions it broadens the life. Everything has its value. Everything has a good use and a bad use. The forces of mind like wealth can be directed either for good or evil. A little rest will re-create forces. Too much rest degenerates into laziness, and brainless, dreamy longings.

If you acquire wealth unjustly from others, you are misusing your forces; but if your wealth comes through the right sources you will be blessed. Through wealth we can do things to uplift ourselves and humanity.

Wealth is many persons' goal. It therefore stimulates their endeavor. They long for it in order to dress and live in such a way as to attract friends. Without friends they would not be so particular of their surroundings. The fact is the more attractive we make ourselves and our surroundings the more inspiring are their influences. It is not conducive to proper thought to be surrounded by conditions that are uncongenial and unpleasant.

So the first step toward acquiring wealth is to surround yourself with helpful influences; to claim for yourself an environment of culture, place yourself in it and be molded by its influences.

Most great men of all ages have been comparatively rich. They have made or inherited money. Without money they could not have accomplished what they did. The man engaged in physical drudgery is not likely to have the same high ideals as the man that can command comparative leisure.

Wealth is usually the fruit of achievement. It is not, however, altogether the result of being industrious. Thousands of persons work hard who never grow wealthy. Others with much less effort acquire wealth. Seeing possibilities is another step toward acquiring wealth. A man may be as industrious as he can possibly be, but if he does not use his mental forces he will be a laborer, to be directed by the man that uses to good advantage his mental forces.

No one can become wealthy in an ordinary lifetime, by mere savings from earnings. Many scrimp and economize all their lives; but by so doing waste all their vitality and energy. For example, I know a man that used to walk to work. It took him an hour to go and an hour to return. He could have taken a car and gone in twenty minutes. He saved ten cents a day but wasted an hour and a half. It was not a very profitable investment unless the time spent in physical exercise yielded him large returns in the way of health.

The same amount of time spent in concentrated effort to overcome his unfavorable business environment might have firmly planted his feet in the path of prosperity.

One of the big mistakes made by many persons of the present generation is that they associate with those who fail to call out or develop the best that is in them. When the social side of life is developed too exclusively, as it often is, and recreation or entertainment becomes the leading motive of a person's life, he acquires habits of extravagance instead of economy; habits of wasting his resources, physical, mental, moral and spiritual, instead of conserving them. He is, in consequence, lacking in proper motivation, his God-given powers and forces are undeveloped and he inevitably brings poor judgment to bear upon all the higher relationships of life, while, as to his financial fortunes, he is ever the leaner; often a parasite, and always, if opportunity affords, as heavy a consumer as he is a poor producer.

It seems a part of the tragedy of life that these persons have to be taught such painful lessons before they can understand the forces and laws that regulate life. Few profit by the mistakes of others. They must experience them for themselves and then apply the knowledge so gained in reconstructing their lives.

Any man that has ever amounted to anything has never done a great deal of detail work for long periods at any given time. He needs his time to reflect. He does not do his duties today in the same way as yesterday, but as the result of deliberate and concentrated effort, constantly tries to improve his methods.

The other day I attended a lecture on Prosperity. I knew the lecturer had been practically broke for ten years. I wanted to hear what he had to say. He spoke very well. He no doubt benefited some of his hearers, but he had not profited by his own teachings. I introduced myself and asked him if he believed in his maxims. He said he did. I asked him if they had made him prosperous. He said not exactly. I asked him why. He answered that he thought he was fated not to experience prosperity.

In half an hour I showed that man why poverty had always been his companion. He had dressed poorly. He held his lectures in poor surroundings. By his actions and beliefs he attracted poverty. He did not realize that his thoughts and his surroundings exercised an unfavorable influence. I said: "Thoughts are moving forces; great powers. Thoughts of wealth attract wealth. Therefore, if you desire wealth you must attract the forces that will help you to secure it. Your thoughts attract a similar kind of thoughts. If you hold thoughts of poverty you attract poverty. If you make up your mind you are going to be wealthy, you will instil this thought into all your mental forces, and you will at the same time use every external condition to help you."

Many persons are of the opinion that if you have money it is easy to make more money. But this is not necessarily true. Ninety per cent of the men that start in business fail. Money will not enable one to accumulate much more, unless he is trained to seek and use good opportunities for its investment. If he inherits money the chances are that he will lose it. While, if he has made it, he not only knows its value, but has developed the power to use it as well as to make more if he loses it.

Business success today depends on foresight, good judgment, grit, firm resolution and settled purpose. But never forget that thought is as real a force as electricity. Let your thoughts be such, that you will send out as good as you receive; if you do not, you are not enriching others, and therefore deserve not to be enriched.

The man that tries to get all he can from others for nothing becomes so selfish and mean that he does not even enjoy his acquisitions. We see examples of this every day. What we take from others, will in turn, be taken from us. All obligations have to be met fairly and squarely. We cannot reach perfection until we discharge every obligation of our lives. We all realize this, so why not willingly give a fair exchange for all that we receive?

Again I repeat that the first as well as the last step in acquiring wealth is to surround yourself with good influences—good thought, good health, good home and business environment and successful business associates. Cultivate, by every legitimate means, the acquaintance of men of big caliber. Bring your thought vibrations in regard to business into harmony with theirs. This will make your society not only agreeable, but sought after, and, when you have formed intimate friendships with clean, reputable men of wealth, entrust to them, for investment, your surplus earnings, however small, until you have developed the initiative and business acumen to successfully manage your own investments. By this time you will, through such associations, have found your place in life which, if you have rightly concentrated upon and used your opportunities, will not be among men of small parts. With a competence secured, you will take pleasure in using a part of it in making the road you traveled in reaching your position easier for those who follow you.

There is somewhere in every brain the energy that will get you out of that rut and put you far up on the mountain of success if you can only use the energy.

You know that gasoline in the engine of an automobile doesn't move the car until the spark comes to explode the gasoline.

So it is with the mind of man. We are not speaking now of men of great genius, but of average, able citizens.

Each one of them has in his brain the capacity to climb over the word impossible and get into the successful country beyond.

And hope, self-confidence and the determination to do something supply the spark that makes the energy work.

# Lesson XIII: You Can Concentrate, but Will You?

All have the ability to concentrate, but will you? You can, but whether you will or not depends on you. It is one thing to be able to do something, and another thing to do it. There is far more ability not used than is used. Why do not more men of ability make something of themselves? There are comparatively few successful men but many ambitious ones. Why do not more get along? Cases may differ, but the fault is usually their own. They have had chances, perhaps better ones than some others that have made good.

What would you like to do, that you are not doing? If you think you should be "getting on" better, why don't you? Study yourself carefully. Learn your shortcomings. Sometimes only a mere trifle keeps one from branching out and becoming a success. Discover why you have not been making good—the cause of your failure. Have you been expecting someone to lead you, or to make a way for you? If you have, concentrate on a new line of thought.

There are two things absolutely necessary for success—energy and the will to succeed. Nothing can take the place of either of these. Most of us will not have an easy path to follow so don't expect to find one. The hard knocks develop our courage and moral stamina. The persons that live in an indolent and slipshod way never have any. They have never faced conditions and therefore don't know how. The world is no better for their living.

We must make favorable conditions and not expect them to shape themselves. It is not the man that says, "It can't be done," but the man that goes ahead in spite of adverse advice, and shows that "it can be done" that "gets there" today. "The Lord helps those that help themselves," is a true saying. We climb the road to success by overcoming obstacles. Stumbling blocks are but stepping stones for the man that says, "I can and I Will." When we see cripples, the deaf and dumb, the blind and those with other handicaps amounting to something in the world, the able-bodied man should feel ashamed of himself if he does not make good.

There is nothing that can resist the force of perseverance. The way ahead of all of us is not clear sailing, but all hard passages can be bridged, if you just think they can and concentrate on how to do it. But if you think the obstacles are unsurmountable, you will not of course try, and even if you do, it will be in only a half-hearted way—a way that accomplishes nothing.

Many men will not begin an undertaking unless they feel sure they will succeed in it. What a mistake! This would be right, if we were sure of what we could and could not do. But who knows? There may be an obstruction there now that might not be there next week. There may not be an obstruction there now that will be there next week. The trouble with most persons is that just as soon as they see their way blocked they lose courage. They forget that usually there is a way around the difficulty. It's up to you to find it. If you tackle something with little effort, when the conditions call for a big effort, you will of course not win. Tackle everything with a feeling that you will utilize all the power within you to make it a success. This is the kind of concentrated effort that succeeds.

Most people are beaten before they start. They think they are going to encounter obstacles, and they look for them instead of for means to overcome them. The result is that they increase their obstacles instead of diminishing them. Have you ever undertaken something that you thought would be hard, but afterwards found it to be easy? That is the way a great many times. The things that look difficult in advance turn out to be easy of conquest when once encountered. So start out on your journey with the idea that the road is going to be clear for you, and that if it is not you will clear the way. All men that have amounted to anything have cleared their way and they did not have the assistance that you will have today.

The one great keynote of success is to do whatever you have decided on. Don't be turned from your path, but resolve that you are going to accomplish what you set out to do. Don't be frightened at a few rebuffs, for they cannot stop the man that is determined—the man that knows in his heart that success is only bought by tremendous resolution, by concentrated and whole-hearted effort.

"He who has a firm will," says Goethe, "molds the world to himself."

"People do not lack strength," says Victor Hugo; "they lack Will."

It is not so much skill that wins victories as it is activity and great determination There is no such thing as failure for the man that does his best. No matter what you may be working at, at the present time, don't let this make you lose courage. The tides are continually changing, and tomorrow or some other day they will turn to your advantage if you are a willing and are an ambitious worker. There is nothing that develops you and increases your courage like work. If it were not for work how monotonous life would at last become!

So I say to the man that wants to advance, "Don't look upon your present position as your permanent one. Keep your eyes open, and add those qualities to your makeup that will assist you when your opportunity comes. Be ever alert and on the watch for opportunities. Remember, we attract what we set our minds on. If we look for opportunities, we find them.

If you are the man you should be, some one is looking for you to fill a responsible position. So when he finds you, don't let your attention wander. Give it all to him. Show that you can concentrate your powers, that you have the makeup of a real man. Show no signs of fear, uncertainty or doubt. The man that is sure of himself is bound to get to the front. No circumstances can prevent him.

# Lesson XIV: The Art of Concentrating by Means of Practical Exercises

Select some thought, and see how long you can hold your mind on it. It is well to have a clock at first and keep track of the time. If you decide to think about health, you can get a great deal of good from your thinking besides developing concentration. Think of health as being the greatest blessing there is, in the world. Don't let any other thought drift in. Just the moment one starts to obtrude, make it get out.

Make it a daily habit of concentrating on this thought for, say, ten minutes. Practice until you can hold it to the exclusion of everything else. You will find it of the greatest value to centralize your thoughts on health. Regardless of your present condition, see yourself as you would like to be and be blind to everything else. You will find it hard at first to forget your ailments, if you have any, but after a short while you can shut out these negative thoughts and see yourself as you want to be. Each time you concentrate you form a more perfect image of health, and, as you come into its realization, you become healthy, strong and wholesome.

I want to impress upon your mind that the habit of forming mental images is of the greatest value. It has always been used by successful men of all ages, but few realize its full importance.

Do you know that you are continually acting according to the images you form? If you allow yourself to mould negative images you unconsciously build a negative disposition. You will think of poverty, weakness, disease, fear, etc. Just as surely as you think of these will your objective life express itself in a like way. Just what we think, we will manifest in the external world.

In deep concentration you become linked with the great creative spirit of the universe, and the creative energy then flows through you, vitalizing your creations into form. In deep concentration your mind becomes attuned with the infinite and registers the cosmic intelligence and receives its messages. You become so full of the cosmic energy that you are literally flooded with divine power. This is a most desired state. It is then we realize the advantages of being connected with the supra-consciousness. The supra-consciousness registers the higher cosmic vibrations. It is often referred to as the wireless station, the message recorded coming from the universal mind.

There are very few that reach this stage of concentration. Very few even know that it is possible. They think concentration means limitation to one subject, but this deeper concentration that brings us into harmony with the Infinite is that which produces and maintains health.

When you have once come in contact with your supra-consciousness you become the controller of your human thoughts. That which comes to you is higher than human thoughts. It is often spoken of as Cosmic Consciousness. Once it is experienced it is never forgotten. Naturally it requires a good deal of training to reach this state, but once you do, it becomes easier each time to do, and in the course of time you can become possessed of power which was unknown to you before. You are able to direct the expression of almost Infinite Power while in this deeper state of concentration.

Exercises In Concentration. The rays of the sun, when focused upon an object by means of a sun glass, produce a heat many times greater than the scattered rays of the same source of light and heat. This is true of attention. Scatter it and you get but ordinary results. But center it upon one thing and you secure much better results. When you focus your attention upon an object your every action, voluntary and involuntary, is in the direction of attaining that object. If you will focus your energies upon a thing to the exclusion of everything else, you generate the force that can bring you what you want.

When you focus your thought, you increase its strength. The exercises that follow are tedious and monotonous, but useful. If you will persist in them you will find they are very valuable, as they increase your powers of concentration.

Before proceeding with the exercises I will answer a question that just comes to me. This person says after he works all day he is too tired to practice any exercise. But this is not true. We will say he comes home all tired out, eats his supper and sits down to rest. If his work has been mental, the thought which has been occupying his mind returns to him and this prevents him from securing the rest he needs.

It is an admitted fact that certain thoughts call into operation a certain set of brain cells; the other cells, of course, are not busy at that time and are rested. Now if you take up something that is just different from what you have been doing during the day, you will use the cells that have not done anything and give those that have had work to do a rest. So you should regulate the evenings that you have and call forth an entirely different line of thought so as not to use the cells which you have tired out during the day. If you will center your attention on a new thought, you relieve the old cells from vibrating with excitement and they get their needed rest. The other cells that have been idle all day want to work, and you will find you can enjoy your evenings while securing needed rest.

When once you have learned to master your thoughts, you will be able to change them just as easily as you change your clothes.

Remember, the real requisite of centering is to be able to shut out outside thoughts—anything foreign to the subject. Now, in order to control your intention first gain control over the body. This must be brought under direct control of the mind; the mind under the control of the will. Your will is strong enough to do anything you wish, but you must realize that it is. The mind can be greatly strengthened by being brought under the direct influence of the will. When the mind is properly strengthened by the impulse of the will it becomes a more powerful transmitter of thought, because it has more force.

The Best Time to Concentrate Is after reading something that is inspiring, as you are then mentally and spiritually exalted in the desired realm. Then is the time you are ready for deep concentration. If you are in your room first see that your windows are up and the air is good. Lie down flat on your bed without a pillow. See that every muscle is relaxed. Now breathe slowly, filling the lungs comfortably full of fresh air; hold this as long as you can without straining yourself; then exhale slowly. Exhale in an easy, rhythmic way. Breathe this way for five minutes, letting the Divine Breath flow through you, which will cleanse and rejuvenate every cell of brain and body.

You are then ready to proceed. Now think how quiet and relaxed you are. You can become enthusiastic over your condition. Just think of yourself as getting ready to receive knowledge that is far greater than you have ever received before. Now relax and let the spirit work in and through you and assist you to accomplish what you wish.

Don't let any doubts or fears enter. Just feel that what you wish is going to manifest. Just feel it already has, in reality it has, for just the minute you wish a thing to be done it manifests in the thought world. Whenever you concentrate just believe it is a success. Keep up this feeling and allow nothing to interfere and you will soon find you have become the master of concentration. You will find that this practice will be of wonderful value to you, and that rapidly you will be learning to accomplish anything that you undertake.

It will be necessary to first train the body to obey the commands of the mind. I want you to gain control of your muscular movements. The following exercise is especially good in assisting you to acquire perfect control of the muscles.

**Exercise 1**

Sit in a comfortable chair and see how still you can keep. This is not as easy as it seems. You will have to center your attention on sitting still. Watch and see that you are not making any involuntary muscular movements. By a little practice you will find you are able to sit still without a movement of the muscles for fifteen minutes. At first I advise sitting in a relaxed position for five minutes. After you are able to keep perfectly still, increase the time to ten minutes and then to fifteen. This is as long as it is necessary. But never strain yourself to keep still. You must be relaxed completely. You will find this habit of relaxing is very good.

**Exercise 2**

Sit in a chair with your head up and your chin out, shoulders back. Raise your right arm until it is on the level with your shoulder, pointing to your right. Look around, with head only, and fix your gaze on your fingers, and keep the arm perfectly still for one minute. Do the same exercise with left arm. When you are able to keep the arm perfectly steady, increase the time until you are able to do this five minutes with each arm. Turn the palm of the hand downward when it is outstretched, as this is the easiest position. If you will keep your eyes fixed on the tips of the fingers you will be able to tell if you are keeping your arm perfectly still.

**Exercise 3**

Fill a small glass full of water, and grasp it by the fingers; put the arm directly in front of you. Now fix the eyes upon the glass and try to keep the arm so steady that no movement will be noticeable. Do this first for one moment and then increase it to five. Do the exercise with first one arm and then the other.

**Exercise 4**

Watch yourself during the day and see that your muscles do not become tense or strained. See how easy and relaxed you can keep yourself. See how poised you can be at all times. Cultivate a self-poised manner, instead of a nervous, strained appearance. This mental feeling will improve your carriage and demeanor. Stop all useless gestures and movements of the body. These mean that you have not proper control over your body. After you have acquired this control, notice how "ill-at-ease" people are that have not gained this control. I have just been sizing up a salesman that has just left me. Part of his body kept moving all the time. I just felt like saying to him, "Do you know how much better appearance you would make if you would just learn to speak with your voice instead of trying to express what you say with your whole body?" Just watch those that interview you and see how they lack poise.

Get rid of any habit you have of twitching or jerking any part of your body. You will find you make many involuntary movements. You can quickly stop any of these by merely centering your attention on the thought, "I will not."

If you are in the habit of letting noises upset you, just exercise control; when the door slams, or something falls, etc., just think of these as exercises in self-control. You will find many exercises like this in your daily routine.

The purpose of the above exercises is to gain control over the involuntary muscular movement, making your actions entirely voluntary. The following exercises are arranged to bring your voluntary muscles under the control of the will, so that your mental forces may control your muscular movements.

### Exercise 5
Move your chair up to a table, placing your hands upon it, clenching the fists, keeping the back of the hand on the table, the thumb doubled over the fingers. Now fix your gaze upon the fist for a while, then gradually extend the thumb, keeping your whole attention fixed upon the act, just as if it was a matter of great importance. Then gradually extend your first finger, then your second and so on until you open the rest. Then reverse the process, closing first the last one opened and then the rest, and finally you will have the fist again in the original position with the thumb closed over the finger. Do this exercise with the left hand. Keep up this exercise first with one hand and then the other until you have done it five times with each hand. In a few days you can increase it to ten times.

The chances are that the above exercises will at first make you "tired," but it is important for you to practice these monotonous exercises so you can train your attention. It also gives you control over your muscular movement. The attention, of course, must be kept closely on each movement of the hand; if it is not, you of course lose the value of the exercise.

### Exercise 6
Put the right hand on knee, both fingers and thumb closed, except the first finger, which points out in front of you. Then move the finger slowly from side to side, keeping the attention fixed upon the end of the finger. You can make up a variety of exercises like these. It is good training to plan out different ones. The main point you should keep in

mind is that the exercise should be simple and that the attention should be firmly fixed upon the moving part of the body. You will find your attention will not want to be controlled and will try to drift to something more interesting. This is just where these exercises are of value, and you must control your attention and see it is held in the right place and does not wander away.

You may think these exercises very simple and of no value, but I promise you in a short time you will notice that you have a much better control over your muscular movements, carriage and demeanor, and you will find that you have greatly improved your power of attention, and can center your thoughts on what you do, which of course will be very valuable.

No matter what you may be doing, imagine that it is your chief object in life. Imagine you are not interested in anything else in the world but what you are doing. Do not let your attention get away from the work you are at. Your attention will no doubt be rebellious, but control it and do not let it control you. When once you conquer the rebellious attention you have achieved a greater victory than you can realize at the time. Many times afterwards you will be thankful you have learned to concentrate your closest attention upon the object at hand.

Let no day go by without practicing concentrating on some familiar object that is uninteresting. Never choose an interesting object, as it requires less attention. The less interesting it is the better exercise will it be. After a little practice you will find you can center your attention on uninteresting subjects at will.

The person that can concentrate can gain full control over his body and mind and be the master of his inclinations; not their slave. When you can control yourself you can control others. You can develop a Will that will make you a giant compared with the man that lacks Will Power. Try out your Will Power in different ways until you have it under such control that just as soon as you decide to do a thing you go ahead and do it. Never be satisfied with the "I did fairly well" spirit, but put forward your best efforts. Be satisfied with nothing else. When you have gained this you are the man you were intended to be.

### Exercise 7

Concentration Increases the Sense of Smell. When you take a walk, or drive in the country, or pass a flower garden, concentrate on the odor of flowers and plants. See how many different kinds you can detect. Then choose one particular kind and try to sense only this. You will find that this strongly intensifies the sense of smell. This differentiation requires, however, a peculiarly attentive attitude. When sense of smell is being developed, you should not only shut out from the mind every thought but that of odor, but you should also shut out cognizance of every odor save that upon which your mind, for the time, is concentrated.

You call find plenty of opportunity for exercises for developing the sense of smell. When you are out in the air, be on the alert for the different odors. You will find the air laden with all kinds, but let your concentration upon the one selected be such that a scent of its fragrance in after years will vividly recall the circumstances of this exercise.

The object of these exercises is to develop concentrated attention, and you will find that you can, through their practice, control your mind and direct your thoughts just the same as you can your arm.

### Exercise 8

Concentration on the Within. Lie down and thoroughly relax your muscles. Concentrate on the beating of your heart. Do not pay any attention to anything else. Think how this great organ is pumping the blood to every part of the body; try to actually picture the blood leaving the great reservoir and going in one stream right down to the toes. Picture another going down the arms to the tips of the fingers. After a little practice you can actually feel the blood passing through your system.

If, at any time, you feel weak in any part of the body, will that an extra supply of blood shall go there. For instance, if your eyes feel tired, picture the blood coming from the heart, passing up through the head and out to the eyes. You can wonderfully increase your strength by this exercise. Men have been able to gain such control over the heart that they have actually stopped it from beating for five minutes. This, however, is not without danger, and is not to be practiced by the novice.

I have found the following a very helpful exercise to take just before going to bed and on rising in the morning: Say to yourself, "Every cell in my body thrills with life; every part of my body is strong and healthy." I have known a number of people to greatly improve their health in this way. You become what you picture yourself to be. If your mind thinks of sickness in connection with self you will be sick. If you imagine yourself in strong, vigorous health, the image will be realized. You will be healthy.

### Exercise 9

Concentrating on Sleep. What is known as the water method is, although very simple, very effective in inducing sleep.

Put a full glass of clear water on a table in your sleeping room. Sit in a chair beside the table and gaze into the glass of water and think how calm it is. Then picture yourself, getting into just as calm a state. In a short time you will find the nerves becoming quiet and you will be able to go to sleep. Sometimes it is good to picture yourself becoming drowsy to induce sleep, and, again, the most persistent insomnia has been overcome by one thinking of himself as some inanimate object—for instance, a hollow log in the depths of the cool, quiet forest.

Those who are troubled with insomnia will find these sleep exercises that quiet the nerves very effective. Just keep the idea in your mind that there is no difficulty in going to sleep; banish all fear of insomnia. Practice these exercises and you will sleep.

By this time you should have awakened to the possibilities of concentration and have become aware of the important part it plays in your life.

### Exercise 10
Concentration Will Save Energy and Appearance. Watch yourself and see if you are not in the habit of moving your hands, thumping something with your fingers or twirling your mustache. Some have the habit of keeping their feet going, as, for instance, tapping them on the floor. Practice standing before a mirror and see if you are in the habit of frowning or causing wrinkles to appear in the forehead. Watch others and see how they needlessly twist their faces in talking. Any movement of the face that causes the skin to wrinkle will eventually cause a permanent wrinkle. As the face is like a piece of silk, you can make a fold in it a number of times and it will straighten out of itself, but, if you continue to make a fold in it, it will in time be impossible to remove it.

By Concentration You Can Stop the Worry Habit. If you are in the habit of worrying over the merest trifles, just concentrate on this a few minutes and see bow needless it is; if you are also in the habit of becoming irritable or nervous at the least little thing, check yourself instantly when you feel yourself becoming so; start to breathe deeply; say, "I will not be so weak; I am master of myself," and you will quickly overcome your condition.

### Exercise 11
By Concentration You Can Control Your Temper. If you are one of those that flare up at the slightest "provocation" and never try to control yourself, just think this over a minute. Does it do you any good? Do you gain anything by it? Doesn't it put you out of poise for some time? Don't you know that this grows on you and will eventually make you despised by all that have any dealings with you? Everyone makes

mistakes and, instead of becoming angry at their perpetrators, just say to them, "Be more careful next time." This thought will be impressed on them and they will be more careful. But, if you continually complain about their making a mistake, the thought of a mistake is impressed on them and they will be more likely to make mistakes in the future. All lack of self-control can be conquered if you will but learn to concentrate.

Many of you that read this may think you are not guilty of either of these faults, but if you will carefully watch yourself you will probably find that you are, and, if so, you will be greatly helped by repeating this affirmation each morning:

"I am going to try today not to make a useless gesture or to worry over trifles, or become nervous or irritable. I intend to be calm, and, no difference what may be the circumstances, I will control myself. Henceforth I resolve to be free from all signs that show lack of self-control."

At night quickly review your actions during the day and see how fully you realized your aim. At first you will, of course, have to plead guilty of violation a few times, but keep on, and you will soon find that you can live up to your ideal. After you have once gained self-control, however, don't relinquish it. For some time it will still be necessary to repeat the affirmation in the morning and square your conduct with it in the evening. Keep up the good work until, at last, the habit of self-control is so firmly fixed that you could not break it even though you tried.

I have had many persons tell me that this affirmation and daily review made a wonderful difference in their lives. You, too, will notice the difference if you live up to these instructions.

Exercise 12.

Practice Talking Before a Glass. Make two marks on your mirror on a level with your eyes, and think of them as two human eyes looking into yours. Your eyes will probably blink a little at first. Do not move your head, but stand erect. Concentrate all your thoughts on keeping your head perfectly still. Do not let another thought come into your mind. Then, still keeping the head, eyes and body still, think that you look like a reliable man or woman should; like a person that anyone would have confidence in. Do not let your appearance be such as to justify the remark, "I don't like his appearance. I don't believe he can be trusted."

While standing before the mirror practice deep breathing. See that there is plenty of fresh air in the room, and that you are literally feasting on it. You will find that, as it permeates every cell, your timidity will disappear. It has been replaced by a sense of peace and power.

The one that stands up like a man and has control over the muscles of his face and eyes always commands attention. In his conversation, he can better impress those with whom he comes in contact. He acquires a feeling of calmness and strength that causes opposition to melt away before it.

Three minutes a day is long enough for the practice of this exercise.

Look at the clock before you commence the exercise, and if you find you can prolong the exercise for more than five minutes do so. The next day sit in a chair and, without looking at the picture, concentrate on it and see if you cannot think of additional details concerning it. The chances are you will be able to think of many more. It might be well for you to write down all you thought of the first day, and then add to the list each new discovery. You will find that this is a very excellent exercise in concentration.

### Exercise 13

The Control of Sensations. Think how you would feel if you were cool; then how you would feel if you were cold; again, how you would feel if it were freezing. In this state you would be shivering all over. Now think of just the opposite conditions; construct such a vivid image of heat that you are able to experience the sensation of heat even in the coldest atmosphere. It is possible to train your imagination until you do this, and it can then be turned to practical account in making undesirable conditions bearable.

You can think of many very good exercises like this. For instance, if you feel yourself getting hungry or thirsty and for any reason you do not wish to eat, do not think of how hungry or thirsty you are, but just visualize yourself as finishing a hearty meal. Again, when you experience pain, do not increase it by thinking about it, but do something to divert your attention, and the pain will seem to decrease. If you will start practicing along this line systematically you will soon gain a wonderful control over the things that affect your physical comfort.

### Exercise 14

The Eastern Way of Concentrating. Sit in a chair with a high back in upright position. Press one finger against the right nostril. Now take a long, deep breath, drawing the breath in gently as you count ten; then expel the breath through the right nostril as you count ten. Repeat this exercise with the opposite nostril. This exercise should be done at least twenty times at each sitting.

**Exercise 15**

Controlling Desires. Desire, which is one of the hardest forces to control, will furnish you with excellent exercises in concentration. It seems natural to want to tell others what you know; but, by learning to control these desires, you can wonderfully strengthen your powers of concentration. Remember, you have all you can do to attend to your own business. Do not waste your time in thinking of others or in gossiping about them.

If, from your own observation, you learn something about another person that is detrimental, keep it to yourself. Your opinion may afterwards turn out to be wrong anyway, but whether right or wrong, you have strengthened your will by controlling your desire to communicate your views.

If you hear good news resist the desire to tell it to the first person you meet and you will be benefited thereby. It will require the concentration of all your powers of resistance to prohibit the desire to tell. After you feel that you have complete control over your desires you can then tell your news. But you must be able to suppress the desire to communicate the news until you are fully ready to tell it. Persons that do not possess this power of control over desires are apt to tell things that they should not, thereby often involving both themselves and others in needless trouble.

If you are in the habit of getting excited when you hear unpleasant news, just control yourself and receive it without any exclamation of surprise. Say to yourself, "Nothing is going to cause me to lose my self-control. You will find from experience that this self-control will be worth much to you in business. You will be looked upon as a cool-headed business man, and this in time becomes a valuable business asset. Of course, circumstances alter cases. At times it is necessary to become enthused. But be ever on the lookout for opportunities for the practice of self-control. "He that ruleth his spirit is greater than he that ruleth a city."

**Exercise 16**

When You Read. No one can think without first concentrating his thoughts on the subject in hand. Every man and woman should train himself to think clearly. An excellent exercise is to read some short story and then write just an abridged statement. Read an article in a newspaper, and see in how few words you can express it. Reading an article to get only the essentials requires the closest concentration. If you are unable to write out what you read, you will know you are weak in concentration. Instead of writing it out you can express it orally if you wish. Go to your room and deliver it as if you were talking to some one. You will find exercises like this of the greatest value in developing concentration and learning to think.

After you have practiced a number of these simple exercises read a book for twenty minutes and then write down what you have read. The chances are that at first you will not remember very many details, but with a little practice you will be able to write a very good account of what you have read. The closer the concentration the more accurate the account will be.

It is a good idea when time is limited to read only a short sentence and then try to write it down word for word. When you are able to do this, read two or more sentences and treat similarly. The practice will produce very good results if you keep it up until the habit is fixed.

If you will just utilize your spare time in practicing exercises like those suggested you can gain wonderful powers of concentration. You will find that in order to remember every word in a sentence you must keep out every thought but that which you wish to remember, and this power of inhibition alone will more than compensate for the trouble of the exercise. Of course, success in all of the above depends largely upon cultivating, through the closest concentration, the power to image or picture what you read; upon the power, as one writer expresses it, of letting the mountains of which we hear loom before us and the rivers of which we read roll at our feet.

### Exercise 17

Concentration Overcomes Bad Habits. If you have a habit that you want to get rid of, shut your eyes and imagine that your real self is standing before you. Now try the power of affirmation; say to yourself, "You are not a weakling; you can stop this habit if you want to. This habit is bad and you want to break it." Just imagine that you are some one else giving this advice. This is very valuable practice. You, in time, see yourself as others see you. The habit loses its power over you and you are free.

If you will just form the mental image of controlling yourself as another person might, you will take a delight in breaking bad habits. I have known a number of men to break themselves of drinking in this way.

### Exercise 18

Watch Concentration. Sit in a chair and place a clock with a second hand on the table. Follow the second hand with your eyes as it goes around. Keep this up for five minutes, thinking of nothing else but the second hand, This is a very good exercise when you only have a few minutes to spare, if you are able to keep every other thought in the stream of consciousness subordinate to it. As there is little that is particularly interesting about the second hand, it is hard to do this, but in the extra effort of will power required to make it successful lies its value. Always try to keep as still as possible during these exercises.

In this way you can gain control over nerves and this quieting effect is very good for them.

### Exercise 19

Faith Concentration. A belief in the power to concentrate is of course very important. I purposely did not put this exercise in the beginning where it naturally belongs because I wanted you to know that you could learn to concentrate. If you have practiced the above exercises you have now developed this concentration power to a considerable extent and therefore you have faith in the power of concentration, but you can still become a much stronger believer in it.

We will say that you have some desire or wish you want fulfilled, or that you need some special advice. You first clearly picture what is wanted and then you concentrate on getting it. Have absolute faith that your desires will be realized. Believe that it will according to your belief be fulfilled. Never, at this time, attempt to analyze the belief. You don't care anything about the whys and wherefores. You want to gain the thing you desire, and if you concentrate on it in the right way you will get it.

A Caution. Never think you will not succeed, but picture what is wanted as already yours, and yours it surely will be.

Self-Distrust. Do you ever feel distrust in yourself? If You do, just ask yourself, which self do I mistrust? Then say: my higher self cannot be affected. Then think of the wonderful powers of the higher self. There is a way to overcome all difficulties, and it is a delight for the human soul to do so. Instead of wasting precious thought-force by dreading or fearing a disagreeable interview or event, instead devote the time and concentrated thought in how to make the best of the interview or event and you will find that it will not be as unpleasant as you thought it would be. Most of our troubles are but imaginary, and it is the mental habit of so dreading them that really acts as a magnet in attracting those that really do come. Your evil circumstances are created or attracted by your own negative, fears and wrong thoughts, and are a means of teaching you to triumph over all evils, by discovering that which is inherent within yourself.

You will find it helpful in overcoming self-distrust, to stop and think, why you are, concentrating your forces, and by so doing you become more closely attached to the higher self, which never distrusts.

# Lesson XV: Concentrate So You Will Not Forget

A man forgets because he does not concentrate his mind on his purpose, especially at the moment he conceives it. We remember only that which makes a deep impression, hence we must first deepen our impressions by associating in our minds certain ideas that are related to them.

We will say a wife gives her husband a letter to mail. He does not think about it, but automatically puts it in his pocket and forgets all about it. When the letter was given to him had he said to himself, "I will mail this letter. The box is at the next corner and when I pass it I must drop this letter," it would have enabled him to recall the letter the instant he reached the mail box.

The same rule holds good in regard to more important things. For example, if you are instructed to drop in and see Mr. Smith while out to luncheon today, you will not forget it, if, at the moment the instruction is given, you say to yourself something similar to the following:

"When I get to the corner of Blank street, on my way to luncheon, I shall turn to the right and call on Mr. Smith." In this way the impression is made, the connection established and the sight of the associated object recalls the errand.

The important thing to do is to deepen the impression at the very moment it enters your mind. This is made possible, not only by concentrating the mind upon the idea itself, but by surrounding it with all possible association of ideas, so that each one will reinforce the others.

The mind is governed by laws of association, such as the law that ideas which enter the mind at the same time emerge at the same time, one assisting in recalling the others.

The reason why people cannot remember what they want to is that they have not concentrated their minds sufficiently on their purpose at the moment when it was formed.

You can train yourself to remember in this way by the concentration of the attention on your purpose, in accordance with the laws of association.

When once you form this habit, the attention is easily centered and the memory easily trained. Then your memory, instead of failing you at crucial moments, becomes a valuable asset in your every-day work.

Exercise in Memory Concentration. Select some picture; put it on a table and then look at it for two minutes. Concentrate your attention on this picture, observe every detail; then shut your eyes and see how much you can recall about it. Think of what the picture represents; whether it is a good subject; whether it looks natural. Think of objects in foreground, middle ground, background; of details of color and form. Now open your eyes and hold yourself rigidly to the correction of each and every mistake. Close eyes again and notice how much more accurate your picture is. Practice until your mental image corresponds in every particular to the original.

Nature is a Wonderful Instructor. But there are very few who realize that when we get in touch with nature we discover ourselves. That by listening to her voice, with that curious, inner sense of ours, we learn the oneness of life and wake up to our own latent powers.

Few realize that the simple act of listening and concentrating is our best interior power, for it brings us into close contact with the highest, just as our other senses bring us into touch with the coarser side of human nature. The closer we live to nature the more developed is this sense. "So called" civilization has over developed our other senses at the expense of this one.

Children unconsciously realize the value of concentration—for instance: When a Child has a difficult problem to solve, and gets to some knotty point which he finds himself mentally unable to do—though he tries his hardest—he will pause and keep quite still, leaning on his elbow, apparently listening; then you will see, if you are watching, sudden illumination come and he goes on happily and accomplishes his task. A child instinctively but unconsciously knows when he needs help, he must be quiet and concentrate.

All great people concentrate and owe their success to it. The doctor thinks over the symptoms of his patient, waits, listens for the inspiration, though quite unconscious, perhaps, of doing so. The one who diagnoses in this way seldom makes mistakes. An author thinks his plot, holds it in his mind, and then waits, and illumination comes. If you want to be able to solve difficult problems you must learn to do the same.

# Lesson XVI: How Concentration Can Fulfill Your Desire

"It is a spiritual law that the desire to do necessarily implies the ability to do."

You have all read of "Aladdin's Lamp," which accomplished such wonderful things. This, of course, is only a fairy story, but it illustrates the fact that man has within him the power, if he is able to use it, to gratify his every wish.

If you are unable to satisfy your deepest longings it is time you learned how to use your God-given powers. You will soon be conscious that you have latent powers within capable when once developed of revealing to you priceless knowledge and unlimited possibilities of success.

Man should have plenty of everything and not merely substance to live on as so many have. All natural desires can be realized. It would be wrong for the Infinite to create wants that could not be supplied. Man's very soul is in his power to think, and it, therefore, is the essence of all created things. Every instinct of man leads to thought, and in every thought there is great possibility because true thought development, when allied to those mysterious powers which perhaps transcend it, has been the cause of all the world's true progress.

In the silence we become conscious of "that something" which transcends thought and which uses thought as a medium for expression. Many have glimpses of "that something," but few ever reach the state where the mind is steady enough to fathom these depths. Silent, concentrated thought is more potent than spoken words, for speech distracts from the focusing power of the mind by drawing more and more attention to the without.

Man must learn more and more to depend on himself; to seek more for the Infinite within. It is from this source alone that he ever gains the power to solve his practical difficulties. No one should give up when there is always the resources of Infinity. The cause of failure is that men search in the wrong direction for success, because they are not conscious of their real powers that when used are capable of guiding them.

The Infinite within is foreign to those persons who go through life without developing their spiritual powers. But the Infinite helps only he who helps himself. There is no such thing as a Special "Providence."

Man will not receive help from the Infinite except to the extent that he believes and hopes and prays for help from this great source.

Concentrate on What You Want and Get It. The weakling is controlled by conditions. The strong man controls conditions. You can be either the conqueror or the conquered. By the law of concentration you can achieve your heart's desire. This law is so powerful that that which at first seems impossible becomes attainable.

By this law what you at first see as a dream becomes a reality.

Remember that the first step in concentration is to form a Mental Image of what you wish to accomplish. This image becomes a thought-seed that attracts thoughts of a similar nature. Around this thought, when it is once planted in the imagination or creative region of the mind, you group or build associated thoughts which continue to grow as long as your desire is keen enough to compel close concentration.

Form the habit of thinking of something you wish to accomplish for five minutes each day. Shut every other thought out of consciousness. Be confident that you will succeed; make up your mind that all obstacles that are in your way will be overcome and you can rise above any environment.

You do this by utilizing the natural laws of the thought world which are all powerful.

A great aid in the development of concentration is to write out your thoughts on that which lies nearest your heart and to continue, little by little, to add to it until you have as nearly as possible exhausted the subject.

You will find that each day as you focus your forces on this thought at the center of the stream of consciousness, new plans, ideas and methods will flash into your mind. There is a law of attraction that will help you accomplish your purpose. An advertiser, for instance, gets to thinking along a certain line. He has formed his own ideas, but he wants to know what others think. He starts out to seek ideas and he soon finds plenty of books, plans, designs, etc., on the subject, although when he started he was not aware of their existence.

The same thing is true in all lines. We can attract those things that will help us. Very often we seem to receive help in a miraculous way. It may be slow in coming, but once the silent unseen forces are put into operation, they will bring results so long as we do our part. They are ever present and ready to aid those who care to use them. By forming a strong mental image of your desire, you plant the thought-seed which begins working in your interest and, in time, that desire, if in harmony with your higher nature, will materialize.

It may seem that it would be unnecessary to caution you to concentrate only upon achievement that will be good for you and work no harm to another, but there are many who forget others and their rights, in their anxiety to achieve success. All good things are possible for you to have, but only as you bring your forces into harmony with that law that requires that we mete out justice to fellow travelers as we journey along life's road. So first think over the thing wanted and if it would be good for you to have; say, "I want to do this; I am going to work to secure it. The way will be open for me."

If you fully grasp mentally the thought of success and hold it in mind each day, you gradually make a pattern or mold which in time will materialize. But by all means keep free from doubt and fear, the destructive forces. Never allow these to become associated with your thoughts.

At last you will create the desired conditions and receive help in many unlooked-for ways that will lift you out of the undesired environment. Life will then seem very different to you, for you will have found happiness through awakening within yourself the power to become the master of circumstances instead of their slave.

To the beginner in this line of thought some of the things stated in this book may sound strange, even absurd, but, instead of condemning them, give them a trial. You will find they will work out.

The inventor has to work out his idea mentally before he produces it materially. The architect first sees the mental picture of the house he is to plan and from this works out the one we see. Every object, every enterprise, must first be mentally created.

I know a man that started in business with thirteen cents and not a dollar's worth of credit. In ten years he has built up a large and profitable business. He attributes his success to two things—belief that he would succeed and hard work. There were times when it did not look like he could weather the storm. He was being pressed by his creditors who considered him bankrupt. They would have taken fifty cents on the dollar for his notes and considered themselves lucky. But by keeping up a bold front he got an extension of time when needed. When absolutely necessary for him to raise a certain sum at a certain time he always did it. When he had heavy bills to meet he would make up his mind that certain people that owed him would pay by a certain date and they always did. Sometimes he would not receive their check until the last mail of the day of the extension, and I have known him to send out a check with the prospect of receiving a check from one of his customers the following day. He would have no reason other than his belief in the power of affecting the mind of another by concentration of thought for expecting that check, but rarely has he been disappointed.

Just put forth the necessary concentrated effort and you will be wonderfully helped from sources unknown to you.

Remember the mystical words of Jesus, the Master: "Whatsoever thing ye desire when ye pray, pray as if ye had already received and ye shall have."

# Lesson XVII: Ideals Developed by Concentration

Through our paltry stir and strife, Glows the wished Ideal, And longing molds in clay, what life Carves in the marble real.—Lowell.

We often hear people spoken of as idealists. The fact is we are all idealists to a certain extent, and upon the ideals we picture depends our ultimate success. You must have the mental image if you are to produce the material thing. Everything is first created in the mind. When you control your thoughts you become a creator. You receive divine ideas and shape them to your individual needs. All things of this world are to you just what you think they are. Your happiness and success depend upon your ideals.

You are responsible for every condition you go through, either consciously or unconsciously. The next step you take determines the succeeding step. Remember this; it is a valuable lesson. By concentrating on each step as you go along, you can save a lot of waste steps and will be able to choose a straight path instead of a roundabout road.

Concentrate Upon Your Ideals and They Will Become Material Actualities. Through concentration we work out our ideals in physical life. Your future depends upon the ideals you are forming now. Your past ideals are determining your present. Therefore, if you want a bright future, you must begin to prepare for it today.

If persons could only realize that they can only injure themselves, that when they are apparently injuring others they are really injuring themselves, what a different world this would be!

We say a man is as changeable as the weather. What is meant is his ideals change. Every time you change your ideal you think differently. You become like a rudderless boat on an ocean. Therefore realize the importance of holding to your ideal until it becomes a reality.

You get up in the morning determined that nothing will make you lose your temper. This is your ideal of a person of real strength and poise. Something takes place that upsets you completely and you lose your temper. For the time being you forget your ideal. If you had just thought a second of what a well-poised person implies you would not have become angry. You lose your poise when you forget your ideal. Each time we allow our ideals to be shattered we also weaken our will-power. Holding to your ideals develops will-power. Don't forget this.

Why do so many men fail? Because they don't hold to their ideal until it becomes a mental habit. When they concentrate on it to the exclusion of all other things it becomes a reality.

"I am that which I think myself to be."

Ideals are reflected to us from the unseen spirit. The laws of matter and spirit are not the same. One can be broken, but not the other. To the extent that ideals are kept is your future assured.

It was never intended that man should suffer. He has brought it upon himself by disobeying the laws of nature. He knows them so cannot plead ignorance. Why does he break them? Because he does not pay attention to those ideals flashed to him from the Infinite Spirit.

Life is but one continuous unfoldment, and you can be happy every step of the way or miserable, as you please; it all depends upon how we entertain those silent whisperings that come from we know not where. We cannot hear them with mortal ear, but from the silence they come as if they were dreams, not to you or me alone, but to everyone. In this way the grandest thoughts come to us, to use or abuse. So search not in treasured volumes for noble thoughts, but within, and bright and glowing vision will come to be realized now and hereafter.

You must give some hours to concentrated, consistent, persistent thought. You must study yourself and your weaknesses.

No man gets over a fence by wishing himself on the other side. He must climb.

No man gets out of the rut of dull, tiresome, monotonous life by merely wishing himself out of the rut. He must climb.

If you are standing still, or going backward, there is something wrong. You are the man to find out what is wrong.

Don't think that you are neglected, or not understood, or not appreciated.

Such thoughts are the thoughts of failure.

Think hard about the fact that men who have got what you envy got it by working for it.

Don't pity yourself, criticise yourself.

You know that the only thing in the world that you have got to count upon is yourself.

# Lesson XVIII: Mental Control Through Creation

I attended a banquet of inventors recently. Each inventor gave a short talk on something he thought would be accomplished in the future. Many very much needed things were spoken of. One inventor spoke of the possibilities of wireless telephone. Distance, he said, would shortly be annihilated. He thought we would soon be able to talk to the man in the submarine forty fathoms below the surface and a thousand miles away. When he got through he asked if there were any that doubted what he said. No one spoke up. This was not a case of tactful politeness, as inventors like to argue, but a case where no one present really doubted that the inventor's vision would, in the future, materialize.

These shrewd men, some real geniuses, all thought we would in time be able to talk to those a thousand miles away without media. Now, if we can make an instrument so wonderful that we can send wireless messages a thousand miles, is there any reason why we should not through mental control transmit messages from one person to another? The wireless message should not be as easy to send as the projected thought.

The day will come when all business will employ highly developed persons to send out influences. These influences will be so dominating that employes will be partly controlled by them and so you will profit more and more by your mental powers and depend on them to draw to you all forces of a helpful nature. You will be constantly sending out suggestions to your employes and friends. They will receive these unconsciously, but in case yours is the stronger personality they will carry them out the same as if you had spoken them.

This is being done even today. A finely organized company secures the combined effort of all its men. They may be each doing a different kind of work, but all work to bring about the very best results. The whole atmosphere is impregnated with a high standard of workmanship. Everyone feels he must do his best. He could not be in such surroundings and be satisfied to do anything but his best work.

A business will succeed only to the extent that the efforts of all are co-ordinated towards one result. At least one person is needed to direct all toward the desired end. The person at the head does not have to exactly outline to the others what steps to take, but he must possess the mental power of control over others.

An up-to-date business letter is not written in a casual, commonplace way today. The writer tries to convey something he thinks the receiver will be interested to know. In this way he awakens a responsive spirit. Sometimes just the addition of a word or two will change a letter of the matter-of-fact style to one that compels a response. It is not always what is actually in a letter, but the spirit which it breathes that brings results. That intangible something that defies analysis is the projected thought of the master that brings back the harvest that it claims.

But we should not always claim success for ourselves only. If you are anxious that some friend or relative should succeed, think of this person as becoming successful. Picture him in the position you would like to see him in. If he has a weakness, desire and command that it be strengthened; think of his shortcomings which belong to his negative nature as being replaced by positive qualities. Take a certain part of the day to send him thoughts of an up-building nature. You can in this way arouse his mental powers into activity, and once aroused, they will assert themselves and claim their own.

We can accomplish a great deal more than many of us are ready to believe by sending to another our direct, positive and controlling suggestions of leadership, but whether a man is a success or not is greatly determined by the way he acts on the suggestions he receives.

We either advance or decline. We never stand still. Every time we accomplish something it gives us ability to do greater things. The bigger the attempt undertaken, the greater the things accomplished in the future. As a business grows, the head of the business also has to grow. He must advance and be ever the guiding influence. By his power to control, he inspires confidence in those associated with him. Often employes are superior to their employers in some qualities, and, if they had studied, instead of neglected their development, they could have been employers of more commanding influence than those whom they serve.

Through your mental power you can generate in another enthusiasm and the spirit of success, which somehow furnishes an impetus to do something worth while.

In concentrated mental control, there is a latent power more potent than physical force. The person becomes aware that the attitude of the mind has a power of controlling, directing and governing other forces. He has been placed in an attitude capable of acquiring that which he desires.

All of us no matter how strong we are, are affected by the mental forces of our environment. There is no one that can remain neutral to influences. The mind cannot be freed from the forces of a place. If the environment of your place of business is not helpful, it will be harmful. That is why a change of position will often do a person a great deal of good.

No person was ever intended to live alone. If you are shut up with only your own thoughts you suffer from mental starvation. The mind becomes narrow; the mental powers weaken. Living alone often causes some of the milder forms of insanity. If children do not play with those their own age, but associate with only older people, they will take on the actions of the older people. The same is true of older persons if they associate with people younger than they are. They take on the spirit of youth. If you wish to retain your youth you need the influences of youth. Like attracts like all over the world.

The thought element plays a great part in our lives. Every business must not only command physical effort but it must also command thought effort. There must be co-ordination of thought. All employers should aim to secure employes that think along similar lines. They will work in fuller sympathy with each other. They will better understand each other. This enables them to help each other, which would be utterly impossible if they were not in sympathy with each other. It is this that goes to make up a perfect organization, which directs and influences them toward the one end. Instead of each person being a separate unit, each one is like a spoke in a big wheel. Each member carries his own load, and he would not think of shirking. Anyone working in such an atmosphere could not help turning out his best work.

All great leaders must be able to inspire this co-operative spirit. They first secure assistance through their mental control. They then make their assistants realize the value of mental control. Soon there is a close bond between them; they are working toward a single purpose. They profit by their combined effort. The result is that they accomplish much.

If your business is conducted in the right spirit, you can instill your thoughts and your ideas into your employes. Your methods and ideas become theirs. They don't know it, but your mental forces are shaping their work. They are just as certain to produce results as any physical force in nature.

The up-to-date business man of the future is going to take pains to get his employes to think and reason better. He will not want them to become depressed or discouraged. There is time that instead of being wasted he will endeavor to have them use in concentrated effort that will be profitable to both employer and employed. There must be more of the spirit of justice enter into the business of the future.

There is a firm I know that will not hire an employe until he has filled out an application blank. No doubt those that fill it out think it is foolishness, but it is not. A capable manager can look over this application blank and pretty nearly tell if this person will fit into his management. The main thing he wants to know is the applicant's capacity for efficient co-operative effort. He wants persons that have faith in themselves. He wants them to realize that when they talk of misfortunes and become blue they are likely to communicate the same depressing influence to others. The up-to-date manager wants to guard against hiring employes who will obstruct his success.

You must realize that every moment spent in thinking of your difficulties of the past, every moment spent in bad company is attracting to you all that is bad; is attracting influences that must be shaken off before you can advance.

Many firms prefer to hire employes that never worked before so that they have nothing to unlearn. They are then not trained, but have no bad business habits to overcome. They are more easily guided and grasp the new methods more effectively because they are not contrary to what they have already learned. They are at once started on the right road, and as they co-operate readily they receive the mental support of the management in learning the methods that have been perfected. This inspires confidence in themselves and they soon become efficient and, finally, skilled workers.

Most big business firms today employ efficiency experts. Each day or week they are in a different department. They earn their money because they familiarize persons with very little business experience with plans that has taken the "expert" years of training and much money to perfect.

The attitude we take has a great deal more to do with our success than most of us realize. We must be able to generate those forces that are helpful. There is a wonderful power in the thought rightly controlled and projected and we must through concentration develop this power to the fullest possible extent.

We are surrounded by many forces of which we know but little at present. Our knowledge of these is to be wonderfully increased. Each year we learn more about these psychic forces which are full of possibilities of which we are not even dimly conscious. We must believe in mental control, learn more about it, and use it, if we want to command these higher powers and forces which will unquestionably direct the lives of countless future generations.

# Lesson XIX: A Concentrated Will Development

New Method. You will find in this chapter a most effective and most practical method of developing the will. You can develop a strong one if you want to. You can make your Will a dynamo to draw to you untold power. Exercises are given which will, if practiced, strengthen your will, just as you would strengthen your muscles by athletic exercises.

In starting to do anything, we must first commence with elementary principles. Simple exercises will be given. It is impossible to estimate the ultimate good to be derived from the mental cultivation that comes through these attempts at concentration. Even the simple exercises are not to be thought useless. "In no respect," writes Doctor Oppenheim, "can a man show a finer quality of will-power than in his own private, intimate life." We are all subjected to certain temptations. The Will decides whether we will be just, or unjust; pure of thought; charitable in opinion; forbearing in overlooking other's shortcomings; whether we live up to our highest standard. Since these are all controlled by the Will, we should find time for plenty of exercises for training of the will in our daily life.

You, of course, realize that your will should be trained. You must also realize that to do this requires effort that you alone can command. No one can call it forth for you.

To be successful in these exercises you must practice them in a spirit of seriousness and earnestness. I can show you how to train your will, but your success depends upon your mastery and application of these methods.

New Methods of Will-Training. Select a quiet room where you will not be interrupted; have a watch to determine the time, and a note-book in which to enter observations. Start each exercise with date and time of day.

### Exercise 1

Time decided on. Select some time of the day when most convenient. Sit in a chair and look at the door-knob for ten minutes. Then write down what you experienced. At first it will seem strange and unnatural. You will find it hard to hold one position for ten minutes. But keep as still as you can. The time will seem long for it will probably be the first time you ever sat and did nothing for ten minutes. You will find your thoughts wandering from the door-knob, and you will wonder what there can be in this exercise. Repeat this exercise for six days.

10 P. M. 2nd Day.

Notes. You should be able to sit quieter, and the time should pass more quickly. You will probably feel a little stronger because of gaining a better control of your will. It will brace you up, as you have kept your resolution. 10 P. M. 3rd Day.

Notes. It may be a little harder for you to concentrate on the door-knob as perhaps you had a very busy day and your mind kept trying to revert to what you had been doing during the day. Keep on trying and you will finally succeed in banishing all foreign thoughts. Then you should feel a desire to gain still more control. There is a feeling of power that comes over you when you are able to carry out your will. This exercise will make you feel bigger and it awakens a sense of nobility and manliness. You will say, "I find that I can actually do what I want to and can drive foreign thoughts out. The exercise, I can now see, is valuable."

10 P. M. 4th Day.

Notes. "I found that I could look at the door-knob and concentrate my attention on it at once. Have overcome the tendency to move my legs. No other thoughts try to enter as I have established the fact that I can do what I want to do and do not have to be directed. I feel that I am gaining in mental strength, I can now see the wonderful value of being the master of my own will-force. I know now if I make a resolution I will keep it. I have more self-confidence and can feel my self-control increasing.

10 P. M. 5th Day.

Notes. "Each day I seem to increase the intensity of my concentration. I feel that I can center my attention on anything I wish.

10 P. M. 6th Day.

Notes. "I can instantly center my whole attention on the door-knob. Feel that I have thoroughly mastered this exercise and that I am ready for another."

You have practiced this exercise enough, but before you start another I want you to write a summary of just how successful you were in controlling the flitting impulses of the mind and will. You will find this an excellent practice. There is nothing more beneficial to the mind than to pay close attention to its own wonderful, subtle activities.

### Exercise 2

Secure a package of playing cards. Select some time to do the exercise. Each day at the appointed time, take the pack in one hand and then start laying them down on top of each other just as slowly as you can, with an even motion. Try to get them as even as possible. Each card laid down should completely cover the under one. Do this exercise for six days.

### 1st Day.
Notes. Task will seem tedious and tiresome. Requires the closest concentration to make each card completely cover the preceding one. You will probably want to lay them down faster. It requires patience to lay them down so slowly, but benefit is lost if not so placed. You will find that at first your motions will be jerky and impetuous. It will require a little practice before you gain an easy control over your hands and arms. You probably have never tried to do anything in such a calm way. It will require the closest attention of your will. But you will find that you are acquiring a calmness you never had before. You are gradually acquiring new powers. You recognize how impulsive and impetuous you have been, and how, by using your will, you can control your temperament.

### 2nd Day.
Notes. You start laying the cards down slowly. You will find that by practice you can lay them down much faster. But you want to lay them down slowly and therefore you have to watch yourself. The slow, steady movement is wearisome. You have to conquer the desire of wanting to hurry up. Soon you will find that you can go slowly or fast at will.

### 3rd Day.
Notes. You still find it hard to go slowly. Your will urges you to go faster. This is especially true if you are impulsive, as the impulsive character finds it very difficult to do anything slowly and deliberately. It goes against the "grain." This exercise still is tiresome. But when you do it, it braces you up mentally. You are accomplishing something you do not like to do. It teaches you how to concentrate on disagreeable tasks. Writing these notes down you will find very helpful.

### 4th Day.
Notes. I find that I am beginning to place the cards in a mathematical way. I find one card is not completely covering another. I am getting a little careless and must be more careful. I command my will to concentrate more. It does not seem so hard to bring it under control.

**5th Day.**

Notes. I find that I am overcoming my jerky movements, that I can lay the cards down slowly and steadily. I feel that I am rapidly gaining more poise. I am getting better control over my will each day, and my will completely controls my movements. I begin to look on my will as a great governing power. I would not think of parting with the knowledge of will I have gained. I find it is a good exercise and know it will help me to accomplish my tasks.

**6th Day.**

Notes. I begin to feel the wonderful possibilities of the will. It gives me strength to think of the power of will. I am able to do so much more and better work now, that I realize that I can control my will action. Whatever my task, my will is concentrated on it. I am to keep my will centered there until the task is finished. The more closely and definitely I determine what I shall do, the more easily the will carries it out. Determination imparts compelling force to the will. It exerts itself more. The will and the end act and react on each other.

**7th Day.**

Notes. Now try to do everything you do today faster. Don't hurry or become nervous. Just try to do everything faster, but in a steady manner.

You will find that the exercises you have practiced in retardation have steadied your nerves, and thereby made it possible to increase your speed. The will is under your command. Make it carry out resolutions rapidly. This is how you build up your self-control and your self-command. It is then that the human machine acts as its author dictates.

You certainly should now be able to judge of the great benefit that comes from writing out your introspections each day. Of course you will not have the exact experiences given in these examples, but some of these will fit your case. Be careful to study your experiences carefully and make as true a report as you can. Describe your feelings just as they seem to you. Allow your fancies to color your report and it will be worthless. You have pictured conditions as you see them. In a few months, if you again try the same exercises, you will find your report very much better. By these introspections, we learn to know ourselves better and with this knowledge can wonderfully increase our efficiency. As you become used to writing out your report, it will be more accurate. You thus learn how to govern your impulses, activities and weaknesses.

Each person should try to plan exercises that will best fit his needs. If not convenient for you to practice exercises every day, take them twice or three times a week. But carry out any plan you decide to try. If you cannot devote ten minutes a day to the experiments start with five minutes and gradually increase the time. The exercises given are only intended for examples.

Will Training Without Exercise. There are many people that do not want to take the time to practice exercises, so the following instructions for training the will are given to them.

By willing and realizing, the will grows. Therefore the more you will, the more it grows, and builds up power. No matter whether your task is big or small, make it a rule to accomplish it in order to fortify your will. Form the habit of focusing your will in all its strength upon the subject to be achieved. You form in this way the habit of getting a thing done, of carrying out some plan. You acquire the feeling of being able to accomplish that which lies before you, no matter what it is. This gives you confidence and a sense of power that you get in no other way. You know when you make a resolution that you will keep it. You do not tackle new tasks in a half-hearted way, but with a bold, brave spirit. We know that the will is able to carry us over big obstacles. Knowing this despair never claims us for a victim. We have wills and are going to use them with more and more intensity, thus giving us the power to make our resolutions stronger, our actions freer and our lives finer and better.

The education of the will should not be left to chance. It is only definite tasks that will render it energetic, ready, persevering and consistent. The only way it can be done is by self-study and self-discipline. The cost is effort, time and patience, but the returns are valuable. There are no magical processes leading to will development, but the development of your will works wonders for you because it gives you self-mastery, personal power and energy of character.

Concentration of the Will to Win. The adaptability of persons to their business environment is more a matter of determination than anything else. In this age we hear a good deal of talk about a man's aptitudes. Some of his aptitudes, some of his powers, may be developed to a wonderful extent, but he is really an unknown quality until all his latent powers are developed to their highest possible extent. He may be a failure in one line and a big success in another. There are many successful men, that did not succeed well at what they first undertook, but they profited by their efforts in different directions, and this fitted them for higher things, whereas had they refused to adjust themselves to their environment, the tide of progress would have swept them into oblivion.

My one aim in all my works is to try and arouse in the individual the effort and determination to develop his full capacities, his highest possibilities. One thing I want you to realize at the start, that it is not so much ability, as it is the will to do that counts. Ability is very plentiful, but organizing initiative and creative power are not plentiful. It is easy to get employes, but to get someone to train them is harder. Their abilities must be directed to the work they can do. They must be shown how, while at this work, to conserve their energy and they must be taught to work in harmony with others, for most business concerns are dominated by a single personality.

Concentrating on Driving Force Within. We are all conscious, at times, that we have somewhere within us an active driving force that is ever trying to push us onward to better deeds. It is that "force" that makes us feel determined at times to do something worth while. It is not thought, emotion or feeling. This driving force is something distinct from thought or emotion. It is a quality of the soul and therefore it has a consciousness all its own. It is the "I will do" of the will. It is the force that makes the will concentrate. Many have felt this force working within them, driving them on to accomplish their tasks. All great men and women become conscious that this supreme and powerful force is their ally in carrying out great resolutions.

This driving force is within all, but until you reach a certain stage you do not become aware of it. It is most useful to the worthy. It springs up naturally without any thought of training. It comes unprovoked and leaves unnoticed. Just what this force is we do not know, but we do know that it is what intensifies the will in demanding just and harmonious action.

The ordinary human being, merely as merchandise, if he could be sold as a slave, would be worth ten thousand dollars. If somebody gave you a five thousand dollar automobile you would take very good care of it. You wouldn't put sand in the carburetor, or mix water with the gasoline, or drive it furiously over rough roads, or leave it out to freeze at night.

Are you quite sure that you take care of your own body, your own health, your only real property, as well as you would take care of a five thousand dollar automobile if it were given to you?

The man who mixes whiskey with his blood is more foolish than a man would be if he mixed water with gasoline in his car.

You can get another car; you cannot get another body.

The man who misses sleep lives irregularly—bolts his food so that his blood supply is imperfect. That is a foolish man treating himself as he would not treat any other valuable piece of property.

Do you try to talk with men and women who know more than you do, and do you LISTEN rather than try to tell them what you know?

There are a hundred thousand men of fifty, and men of sixty, running along in the old rut, any one of whom could get out of it and be counted among the successful men if only the spark could be found to explode the energy within them now going to waste.

Each man must study and solve his own problem.

# Lesson XX: Concentration Reviewed

In bringing this book to a close, I again want to impress you with the inestimable value of concentration, because those that lack this great power or, rather that fail to develop it, will generally suffer from poverty and unhappiness and their life's work will most often be a failure, while those that develop and use it will make the most of life's opportunities,

I have tried to make these lessons practical and I am sure that many will find them so. Of course the mere reading of them will not do you a great deal of good, but, if the exercises are practiced and worked out and applied to your own individual case, you should be able to acquire the habit of concentration in such measure as to greatly improve your work and increase your happiness.

But remember the best instruction can only help you to the extent to which you put it into practice. I have found it an excellent idea to read a book through first, and then re-read it, and when you come to an idea that appeals to you, stop and think about it, then if applicable to you, repeat it over and over, that you will be impressed by it. In this way you can form the habit of picking out all the good things you read and these will have a wonderful influence on your character.

In this closing chapter, I want to impress you to concentrate on what you do, instead of performing most of your work unconsciously or automatically, until you have formed habits that give you the mastery of your work and your life powers and forces.

Very often the hardest part of work is thinking about it. When you get right into it, it does not seem so disagreeable. This is the experience of many when they first commence to learn how to concentrate. So never think it a difficult task, but undertake it with the "I Will Spirit" and you will find that its acquirement will be as easy as its application will be useful.

Read the life of any great man, and you will generally find that the dominant quality that made him successful was the ability to concentrate. Study those that have been failures and you will often find that lack of concentration was the cause.

"One thing at a time, and that done will
Is a good rule as I can tell."

All men are not born with equal powers, but it is the way they are used that counts. "Opportunity knocks at every man's door." Those that are successful hear the knock and grasp the chance. The failures believe that luck and circumstances are against them. They always blame someone else instead of themselves for their lack of success. We get what is coming to us, nothing more or less. Anything within the universe is within your grasp. Just use your latent powers and it is yours. You are aided by both visible and invisible forces when you concentrate on either "to do" or "to be."

Everyone is capable of some concentration, for without it you would be unable to say or do anything. People differ in the power to concentrate because some are unable to Will to hold the thought in mind for the required time. The amount of determination used determines who has the strongest will. No one's is stronger than yours. Think of this whenever you go against a strong opponent.

Never say "I can't concentrate today." You can do it just the minute you say "I will." You can keep your thoughts from straying, just the same as you can control your arms. When once you realize this fact, you can train the will to concentrate on anything you wish. If it wanders, it is your fault. You are not utilizing your will. But, don't blame it on your will and say it is weak. The will is just the same whether you act as if it were weak or as if it were strong. When you act as if your will is strong you say, "I can." When you act as if it were weak you say, "I can't." It requires the same amount of effort, in each case.

Some men get in the habit of thinking "I can't" and they fail. Others think "I can" and succeed. So remember, it is for you to decide whether you will join the army of "I can't" or "I can."

The big mistake with so many is that they don't realize that when they say "I can't," they really say, "I won't try." You can not tell what you can do until you try. "Can't" means you will not try. Never say you cannot concentrate, for, when you do, you are really saying that you refuse to try.

Whenever you feel like saying, "I can't," say instead, "I possess all will and I can use as much as I wish." You only use as much as you have trained yourself to use.

An Experiment to Try. Before going to bed tonight, repeat, "I am going to choose my own thoughts, and to hold them as long as I choose. I am going to shut out all thoughts that weaken or interfere; that make me timid. My Will is as strong as anyone's else. While going to work the next morning, repeat this over. Keep this up for a month and you will find you will have a better opinion of yourself. These are the factors that make you a success. Hold fast to them always.

Concentration is nothing but willing to do a certain thing. All foreign thoughts can be kept out by willing that they stay out. You cannot realize your possibilities until you commence to direct your mind. You then do consciously what you have before done unconsciously. In this way you note mistakes, overcome bad habits and perfect your conduct.

You have at times been in a position that required courage and you were surprised at the amount you showed. Now, when once you arouse yourself, you have this courage all the time and it is not necessary to have a special occasion reveal it to you. My object in so strongly impressing this on your mind is to make you aware that the same courage, the same determination that you show at certain exceptionable times you have at your command at all times. It is a part of your vast resources. Use it often and well, in working out the highest destiny of which you are capable.

Final Concentration Instruction. You now realize that, in order to make your life worthy, useful and happy, you must concentrate. A number of exercises and all the needed instruction has been given. It now remains for you to form the highest ideal that you can in the present and live up to that ideal, and try to raise it. Don't waste your time in foolish reading. Select something that is inspiring, that you may become enrapport with those that think thoughts that are worth while. Their enthusiasm will inspire and enlighten you. Read slowly and concentrate on what you are reading. Let your spirit and the spirit of the author commune, and you will then sense what is between the lines—those great things which words cannot express.

Pay constant attention to one and one thing only for a given time and you will soon be able to concentrate. Hang on to that thought ceaselessly until you have attained your object. When you work, let your mind dwell steadily on your task. Think before you speak and direct your conversation to the subject under discussion. Do not ramble. Talk slowly, steadily and connectedly. Never form the hurry habit, but be deliberate in all you do. Assume static attitudes without moving a finger or an eyelid, or any part of your body. Read books that treat of but one continuous subject. Read long articles and recall the thread of the argument. Associate yourself with people who are steady, patient and tireless in their thought, action and work. See how long you can sit still and think on one subject without interruption.

Concentrating on the Higher Self. Father Time keeps going on and on. Every day he rolls around means one less day for you on this planet. Most of us only try to master the external conditions of this world. We think our success and happiness depends on us doing so. These are of course important and I don't want you to think they are not, but I want you to realize that when death comes, only those inherent and acquired qualities and conditions within the mentality—your character, conduct and soul growth—will go with you. If these are what they should be, you need not be afraid of not being successful and happy, for with these qualities you can mold external materials and conditions.

Study yourself. Find Your Strong Points And Make Them Stronger As Well As Yo Weak Ones And Strengthen Them. Study yourself carefully and you will see yourself as you really are.

The secret of accomplishment is concentration, or the art of turning all your power upon just one point at a time.

If you have studied yourself carefully you should have a good line on yourself, and should be able to make the proper interior re-adjustments. Remember first, last, and always, Right thinking and right Living necessarily results in happiness, and it is therefore within your power to obtain happiness. Anyone that is not happy does not claim their birthright.

Keep in mind that some day you are going to leave this world and think of what you will take with you. This will assist you to concentrate on the higher forces. Now start from this minute, to act according to the advice of the higher self in everything you do. If you do, its ever harmonious forces will necessarily insure to you a successful fulfilment of all your life purposes. Whenever you feel tempted to disobey your higher promptings, hold the thought

"My-higher-self-insures-to-me-the-happiness-of-doing-that-which -best-answers-my-true-relations-to-all-others."

You possess latent talents, that when developed and utilized are of assistance to you and others. But if you do not properly use them, you shirk your duty, and you will be the loser and suffer from the consequences. Others will also be worse off if you do not fulfil your obligations.

When you have aroused into activity your thought powers you will realize the wonderful value of these principles in helping you to carry out your plans. The right in the end must prevail. You can assist in the working out of the great plan of the universe and thereby gain the reward, or you can work against the great plan and suffer the consequences. The all consuming fires are gradually purifying all discordant elements. If you choose to work contrary to the law you will burn in its crucible, so I want you to learn to concentrate intelligently on becoming in harmony with your higher self. Hold the thought:

"I-will-live-for-my-best. I-seek-wisdom, self-knowledge, happiness-and-power-to-help-others. I-act-from-the-higher-self, therefore-only-the-best-can-come-to-me. The more we become conscious of the presence of the higher self the more we should try to become a true representative of the human soul in all its wholeness and holiness, instead of wasting our time dwelling on some trifling external quality or defect. We should try to secure a true conception of what we really are so as not to over value the external furnishings. You will then not surrender your dignity or self respect, when others ignorantly make a display of material things to show off. Only the person that realizes that he is a permanent Being knows what the true self is.

www.ingramcontent.com/pod-product-compliance
Lightning Source LLC
LaVergne TN
LVHW011155080426
835508LV00007B/425